To B

May you inner —
landscape be always
glowing —
With much love
& blessings,
always,
Claude

Dancing With My Soul

Claude Ohayon-Budhoo

Sunstar
PUBLISHING LTD.

Dancing With My Soul
By Claude Ohayon-Budhoo
© United States Copyright, Claude Ohayon-Budhoo 1995
Sunstar Publishing, Ltd.
116 North Court Street
Fairfield, Iowa

Art Cover: Chrysta Dizon
Graphic Design: Wayne Slowick
Editing: Elizabeth Pasco and Rod Charles

Library of Congress Catalog Card Number: 95-068464

ISBN 0 - 9638502 - 8 - 8

Readers interested in obtaining further information on the subject
matter of this book are invited to correspond with
The Secretary, Sunstar Publishing, Ltd.
116 North Court Street, Fairfield, Iowa 52556

CONTENTS

Epigraph 5

Acknowledgements 7

Foreword by Margo Mansfield .10

Introduction by Dr. J.Gordon Melton 12

Dedication 14

Preface 17

CHAPTER I—LOST IN A MAZE

Healing Through Meditation and Dreams 23

A Word of Advice to My Gynecologist 27

Freedom 66

Pandora's Box or Aladdin's Lamp

    A Matter of Personal Choice 69

Intuition Versus Reason: An Assertion of Faith 74

CHAPTER II—THE JOLT: FACING MYSELF

The Journey 79

Monologing About the Lord God of my Being 82

My Purposeful Teacher, A Determined Warrior 90

A Weak Woman with the Heart of a Tiger 94

Who Is Ramtha? 99

Socrates' Advice: "Know Thyself" 113

Soliloquy 115

House Cleaning 121

Conversation with my Image .123

Idle Conversation with my Outrageous Self 127

The Power of Silence 132

The Trapezist 136

Who Am I? Dear God, Tell me 138

CHAPTER III—THE COSMOS WITHIN ME:
A NEW UNDERSTANDING

Consciousness 163
My Genealogical Tree 165
Hide and Seek 166
Thoughtful Thoughts or The Birth of a Planet 168
Weaving my Web 171
The Visitor 173
The Present Moment 175
The Street Beggar 178
My Aim in Life 179
Sadness and Joy 180
The Valley of The Gods 181

CHAPTER IV—DANCING WITH MY SOUL

A Toast to the God Within 185
The Sound of Wisdom 186
Within: A Mysterious Word 187
Fluttering Feelings Before Sleep 189
The Muse at Play 191
Tap Dancing 193
I Could Fly 194
Thought Recorder 195
The Composer 196
In the Heart of the Woods 197
A Medallion of Light 198
Celebration 201
The Thoughtful Gardener 203
Waking Up 205
Divine Wedding 208

ABOUT THE AUTHOR 211

WHAT IS SUCCESS?
by Ralph Waldo Emerson

To laugh often and much
To win the respect of intelligent people
And the affection of children;
To earn the appreciation of honest critics
And endure the betrayal of false friends;
To appreciate beauty;
To find the best in others;
To leave the world a bit better,
Whether by a healthy child, a garden patch,
Or a redeemed social condition;
To know even one life has breathed easier
Because you have lived;
This is to have succeeded.

ACKNOWLEDGEMENTS

* To my departed parents, Simon and Tamar Ohayon, who lovingly brought me into this world, I want to express my profound love and gratitude for their unconditional love and unforgettable nurturing.

* With my profound affection and gratitude to my brothers and sisters, Marguerite Florentin, Anna Danan, Marcelle Ohayon, Renee Azoulay, Georgette Weibel, Raphael and David Ohayon, all of whom, from my birth, have showered me with love and affection which gave me a very solid base in life.

* I also want to acknowledge that the greatest blessings in my life are my husband, Davison Budhoo, and our two wonderful children, Patrick and Joelle.

I am indeed blessed by God, providence and fortunate circumstances for the three most important people in my life. Their moral support and unconditional love allowed me to be me, without constraints, without expectations and without demands on their part over the past few years.

It is, indeed, a great blessing to be loved for who and what I am, even though we may not agree on certain subjects.

The love and respect the four of us have for each other helps us to grow and evolve freely, constantly enriching one another with our respective pursuits, even if those pursuits do not fall into the category of general acceptance.

And though we do not live under the same roof, not even under the same sky, for our respective pursuits carry us in different parts of the world, we are daily and fully in each other's heart and consciousness and in constant and frequent communication with each other.

The separation exists only geographically. For we are, indeed, an integral part of each other's life. The bond that exists between us, is a bond of unconditional love. It is the love that asks no question. It is the love that understands and knows.

I count my blessings every day for having such a family.

* My heartfelt thanks and great respect to Rodney Charles. When I first heard his voice on the telephone it triggered a feeling of recognition. What did I recognize? A gentleness of being, a very attentive and open-minded individual. In his capacity as Publisher/Editor of my book, he has shown a tireless patience, flexibility and profound insight.

Rodney Charles, the author of *Every Day a Miracle Happens*, made me realize that in today's chaotic and confusing world, it is indeed a miracle to know and interact with people who, like him, display such a great capacity for compassion and understanding.

* Many thanks to Elizabeth Pasco, whose editing skills, brilliant comments and feedback inspired me to write some additional essays that greatly enhanced this book.

* My deep thanks and respect to Dr. Gordon Melton who showed an interest in my book and took the time from his busy schedule to write and comment on this book.

* My profound gratitude and love to Seth, the Entity channeled by Jane Roberts, whose extraordinary books gave me a glimpse at a new reality and perspective on life that ultimately led me to Ramtha's School of Enlightenment.

* I am deeply grateful to J.Z. Knight, who channels Ramtha, for

her dedication to our school. Her fortitude and steadfastness, her dedication to facilitate Ramtha's teaching for nearly two decades, have allowed many students like me to learn, evolve and acquire a greater sense of Self.

* I want to express my deep gratitude to a dear friend of mine, Helen Monteil, who, over the years, has always mirrored back to me love, respect and unconditional acceptance. She always saw me in a grander light than I saw myself. Her vast knowledge has greatly enriched my life. In her company I experience a genuine friendship and a sense of freedom and joy.

* To my friend Ramona Serrato whose inner child is alive and well. Her lively nature constantly displays a no-nonsense approach to life which I greatly admire. Just by being herself, she teaches and reminds me what simplicity is all about.

* My thanks and gratitude to B.J. Lemke, who urged me from the beginning to put my writings into a book form. Thanks B.J. for your encouragement, comments, insights and valuable feedback regarding the practical aspect of this book.

* My deep appreciation to Margo Mansfield who has generously given her time, in spite of her busy schedule, and whose profound insight and comments have contributed to enhance the presentation of this book.

*Finally, I want to give my heartfelt thanks, and my love, to Claude Ohayon-Budhoo, for typing the whole manuscript, diligently and joyfully.

Thank you Claude!

FOREWORD
by Margo Mansfield,
President of Consulting Associates International Inc.,
author/executive producer of Management by Virtue, seminar/video

Into my office came a beautiful woman surrounded by a mist of extraordinary radiance. Her charm was highlighted with an accent of effervescence. As I studied the essence of her being, I was drawn to the depth of wisdom which peered through her eyes. I knew that she was an interesting individual and I knew that the manuscript she had brought me would not be ordinary.

As our conversation grew in substance, I became more intrigued with the vastness of her experiences in life, the gentleness of her experiences in life, the gentleness of her spirit, and her devotion to attaining sovereignty and freedom in her own life.

I began to see that Claude's life had carried her through adventures that were both common and profound. Her common side had led a life of the known and the traditional—growing up, getting married to become the support to a successful husband and mothering secure and accomplished children. Yet, breathing through the placid surface of her life were experiences that created an extraordinary facet of her character. This was the part of Claude that paid homage to her ever-present Spirit, which often wept in pain and sorrow in her search for truth and freedom in a world that honored neither. As she talked, I was clear that it was indeed this very part of her that formed the core of her aliveness.

Claude had one last frontier to explore on her journey—the acceptance of her grand genius in total—the knowingness of genuine self-love. I knew that through the experiences Claude was encountering as she brought her book to the eyes of the world, she would complete her search for self-love. She was almost there as the book was finished—a statement to the world of her worth.

Before leaving, Claude handed me her manuscript. That night I took it to bed with me and became totally engrossed. Its contents drew forth in me the whole spectrum of emotions—laughter, sadness, joy, anger—as her words pulled forth reflections of my own experiences in life.

Claude is led inward through the loving, truthful, gentle, and wise guidance of "Ramtha, the Enlightened One." As Claude speaks to this "inner" journey, which holds the greatest of all treasures, she touches the Divine Mind and loving heart that quickly heals the Soul of the wounds and bruises of the past, as its desire for Love and Joy is acknowledged at last.

In today's world of change and confusion, I am honored to be presenting Claude's words of wisdom to enrich the evolutionary journey of the like-minded. The reader will know Claude as they read this extraordinary work of art but, more than this they will know their own "Self" in a deeper and more compassionate manner—Claude's gift to the world!

INTRODUCTION
by J. Gordon Melton, Ph. D.
Author of *The Encyclopedia of American Religions* and
Director of The Institute for the Study of American Religions

Claude Ohayon-Budhoo's book, *Dancing With My Soul,* tells a universal story. She reached her middle years having attained what many women say they want: a spacious suburban home, two children in college, and a successful husband. Yet, in her passing moments of contemplation, she began to question her life and concluded that she had passed much of it in unawareness, that she was caught in a sense of emptiness. Her life lacked meaning. But there was one resource. She had frequently moved, geographically, in her life, so she concluded that she could risk one more journey—an exploratory journey to her inner territory.

The trip led her to the New Age, to the books of Seth, and finally to Ramtha, the channeled entity who speaks through J.Z. Knight. As a result of her initial decision, Claude's life underwent a transformation from a life in which other people guided her and impersonal structures imposed a world view, to one in which she gained a sense of self-empowerment, of having control over her life. Integral to that new life was an image of womanhood that unites an understanding of femininity and power.

Claude's transformation begins in an act of selfishness, of self-assertion, of the grasp of a personal truth. First, the Seth books opened the possibility of an alternative path. Then, she encountered Ramtha, who became her guru, the real catalyst for change, the one who pushed her into the new life she has finally perceived. She understood the essential teacher-student relationship. She didn't simply copy the teacher, she allowed the teacher to facilitate her discovery of all the resources in her life. And the transformation has continued and matured into a celebration of a new inner life. She has discovered the joy of her journey—through her inner self to her God.

All who have glimpsed some need for change in their life, or who have begun an inner search, or have already become familiar with the hidden territory of the Self, will resonate with and identify with Claude's emergence as a soulful dancer.

DEDICATION

This book is dedicated to "Ramtha, the Enlightened One," who taught me to see myself the way he saw me. A consciousness on a par with his, endowed with equal beauty, wisdom, love, and joy.

He showed me how to dive deep within to be able to shed light and bring those attributes to my awareness.

So, I plunged head on, getting many bruises, heartaches, nausea, and dizziness in the process. But, along the way, I managed, somehow, to dissolve much of my guilt, fears, and poor self-esteem that kept the light concealed from me.

He empowered me by handing to me a double-edged sword. Very difficult to handle, I might add. On one side, I am the master and creator of my own reality. On the other side, everything that pertains to me is of my own doing. That particular edge didn't feel very comfortable at first. For it was easier for me to shy away from my own responsibilities, and accuse everyone I knew for my problems, short-comings, and sad predicaments.

Nay, nay, said Ramtha. Your joy and sorrows spring from you, and you alone. You project it all out there. If you don't like it, change it. You alone are responsible.

Alone, indeed. How cold it felt. How incredibly heavy, and burdensome to be absolutely responsible for my thoughts, and deeds. Absolutely responsible for me.

"You can't be serious, Ramtha!"

"Oh yes, I am," said he.

Change equated paralysis to me. For a while I refused to budge. How could I budge from the feeling deeply entrenched in me that I was a victim of fate? Woe is me. Yeah, I had problems alright, but that's because it was done to me. Don't you know? My parents, the government, religious institutions, the community, the mass media, the dogs in the street, the neighbors' cats, the aliens, it was all their fault. What else? My husband had to be this, my children that, my background family the other, my friends and foes something else.

The whole world had to change, not me.

In retrospect, it sounds quite hilarious. Hilarious indeed.

My resistance to change was formidable. For a while that resistance made me even more stubborn. But not as stubborn as the relentless wind blowing at my consciousness with a perseverance I was no match for. It was Ramtha, the Enlightened One, alias "Lord of the Wind." The more stubborn I was, the harder he blew my way and magnified my wrong postures and fears of all kinds.

So, I finally moved the lenses of my consciousness and focused on my attitude. The glare of my attitude blinded me. I couldn't see a thing. I was overwhelmed by the magnitude of my ignorance and blindness.

With the powerful wind at my back to help me along, I started the long and painful process of untying the knots and inner conflicts that had kept me blind for so long and had made me oblivious to my own attitude. Through this process, a gradual change developed in me. With a strong resolve, mixed with a lot of fear, I opened my Pandora's box, and proceeded to examine and clean it. Examine and empty it.

I realized, somewhere along the way, that I had been afraid of fear itself. That indeed my problems and sorrows were created by my attitude. Looking at the content of that ominous box was not nearly as frightening as the process of opening it up. Once I ventured one toe into its murky waters, it became relatively easy to dive in, if a little disheartening. I thank you, Ramtha, for forcing me to see what I refused to see.

Thank you for teaching me how to transform my Pandora's box

into an Aladdin's lamp. I see better now. I still have a long way to go, for there are still some unexplored and hidden dark corridors within. But, beloved Ramtha, you have paved the way for me to pursue my self-enlightenment.

Your formidable patience showed me that everything was possible. Your formidable compassion showed me also that you did not give up on me. Mainly because, somehow, I never gave up on myself. Never will.

And who knows, maybe one day I will also be able to call myself "Claude the Enlightened One".

I pay homage to you.

I salute you, beloved Ramtha, with a depth of gratitude I have no words for.

I salute you with profound respect and love.

For the essence of your Being, for the beauty of your wisdom, for the magnitude of your Consciousness that let me guess and presume that perhaps one day my Consciousness would be on a par with yours. That let me guess, through the contemplation of your consciousness, the potential of mine.

Over the past five years or so, I have been incubating in stillness and silence. In the process, echoes emerged as well as iridescent bubbles that, from the depth of my being, rose all the way to the surface of my awareness.

I dedicate those bubbles to you, Ramtha, as a testimony to the blessing and profound change your teaching brought to my life. As a token of my love and appreciation for the powerful Consciousness that is YOU.

PREFACE

Sipping a cup of coffee in my kitchen one morning, I looked around and suddenly felt like an alien in my own home. An elegant, spacious home in the suburbs which appeared, at that moment, odd and unreal.

My husband was on a mission overseas, my children in college. Twenty-five years of my life just passed by like the blinking of an eye, and I suddenly landed in a foreign territory that I had no desire or courage to explore. My Self.

All kinds of questions popped into my head, buzzing around like flies, chasing one another, and turning in circle in a dizzying and frantic dance.

Who am I? What is life all about?

Was I dreaming, or were those past twenty-five years real?

What is reality, anyway?

What is dream? And what is the difference?

Where do I look for answers?

Where do I go from here? What do I do now?

I might as well have chased puffs of smoke, because the answers were a deafening silence, engulfing me further in a deeper emptiness. A vast nothingness in which I was unable to grasp or hold on to anything. Yet, I couldn't remain there. I had to do something. I had to propel myself somewhere. Anywhere.

Well, maybe this voyage is inevitable. After all, I resided in eleven different countries in those twenty-five years. What is the problem with one more trip?

This one is definitely a challenge. So, where do I find a guide to help me explore my inner and obscure territory?

Like a sleepwalker, I changed my clothes, pulled my car out of the garage and drove out with no particular destination in mind. For some strange reason, I found myself in front of a New Age book store. Of all places! I had no idea what I was looking for. I went in. Half-heartedly I picked up two or three books.

"You have been here before" read one title. Yeah? So, why am I here again? "Cosmic Awareness" read another. Wonderful! That's all I need! I didn't have the foggiest idea what my role was in the society in which I lived, let alone my relation to the Cosmos! Really!

I was about to leave when a book caught my attention. I picked it up: "The Nature of Personal Reality" by Seth. I opened it randomly: "Where You and the World Meet." My intuition whispered: "Buy it!" I did, and went home with my purchase.

Then my adventure in consciousness started. A grand and painful journey into the unknown. Myself. "The Nature of Personal Reality" was the first book that launched me into an intensive self-quest, leading me, eventually, into self-discovery.

I read all the books channeled by Seth. As I progressed in my reading, I suddenly became aware that all my life I had lived in a dense fog, a sort of blindness that concealed the light and truth. Those books offered a world view that I had no knowledge of up till now. Those books brought forth information that I never learned about in any school. A knowledge that society, I sensed, had hidden from me. It was a freeing knowledge that resonated deep in my heart. It was a knowledge that made eminent sense to me, indeed. And society with its heavy programming, I discovered later, was intent on keeping me on a tight leash.

So, after reading Seth's books which, in retrospect, were a palatable appetizer, I went looking for the main course, the full meal, from one New Age book store to the next. For those books worked up a formidable appetite in me. A hunger to know more and to understand. To make sense of the world out there and the world within me.

And that's how I discovered "Ramtha the Enlightened One." The most outrageous catalyst for my growth to date. The boldest tactician whose books first, and teaching subsequently, would catapult me beyond my personal limitations. Spelling out for me what is real and what is not. Daring me to measure up to the challenge of finding my own answers, and deciding for myself on the merit of his challenging questions and teaching.

My life has never been the same since I enrolled in Ramtha's School of Enlightenment. Through Ramtha's teaching, I gradually began the long, arduous and gratifying process of putting together the pieces of my personal puzzle. Learning to turn my own questions into answers. Understanding that the answers pertaining to my life were nowhere else but within me.

Through Ramtha's teaching I started to reevaluate my personal life, as well as my relationship to society. I started to put two and two together and began to understand the complex and intricate web, the formidable trap of social programming. The incredible jail that social structure constitutes.

The more I understood, the angrier I became.

No wonder I was out of touch with myself. Society's programming made sure of that.

Suddenly, society didn't make much sense any more. I now saw it as a formidable trap in which the individual is entangled like a fly in a spider web. I had to distance myself from it. To vent off my anger and make sense of my life. To come to terms with it. The only way I could do that was to write it down, verbalize and spell it out to myself. I did.

I laid down the voice of logic and reason, the chattering mouth of the intellect, and allowed full expression of the voice of intuition. Intuition whose language is feeling and emotion. Indeed, the language of the heart. An authentic understanding, to be sure.

A miraculous cleansing ensued that radically transformed my life and outlook. I developed a detachment that brought an evenness of being, a greater understanding about society in general, and myself in particular. A healing process that made me come full circle with society. Full circle with me.

But most important of all, I learned to get in touch with what was missing all along. God. Not God out there; not God of any religion, but God within me. The Spirit in me that kept the fire going from one challenge to the next. The awesome and enigmatic Spirit within me that I frantically searched for all over the world—enquiring and questioning Scriptures and religious denominations of every kind—like an absent-minded individual, literally, looking everywhere for my eye-glasses which were perched on my nose all that time. My beautiful Spirit who patiently waited for me to wake up from my deep slumber.

I finally understood that all the obstacles and challenges in my life were a blessing in disguise. That being part of society, any society, is indeed an individual's challenge. For it entailed being thrown into the fire of daily life. By striving and overcoming that fire, one, inevitably, became purified and much stronger.

All the challenges, and grand detours in my life, led me to a door. I pushed it open, entered it, and therein made contact with that which I Am.

This book is the account of my personal meandering, leading me to self-discovery.

The discovery that no one in the world can provide me with joy, or happiness. I can only derive it from myself. Anything, or anyone else in my life is a simple reflection of that fact; a simple projection of my thoughts and expectations.

This book is about self-acknowledgement. It is also about integration. For, there is no separation between Self and the others. In a greater understanding, everyone else is an integral part of me.

Whatever I see, feel, perceive, experience and understand is a projection of me. It is a facet of that which I am.

The more I absorb, the more I expand. The more I expand, the more I integrate in an all-encompassing way. Projecting back to the world a sense of unity, a greater sense of integrity.

As Within, so Without.

Finally, when I finished writing this book, a critic told me that I talk too much about Ramtha. That, perhaps, this book would have more credibility if I didn't mention or quote Ramtha at all. As it is, people might think that I am in a cult or being brainwashed.

I wish to state here that I did not reach this point in my consciousness to be ashamed of my choices. In the past, my choices were never really mine. For, I was influenced by, and took into consideration, all kinds of outside factors and pressures.

Today, I make my choices fully conscious. Singlemindedly, unapologetically, unashamedly so. I am who I am. I love what I have become. For the first time in my life I can proudly say that I am very happy to be me.

If certain people do not agree with what I think or feel, with what I do, that is indeed their prerogative. I fully respect their opinion. It is their own perception and truth. But it has no bearing on what I think or do. For, that is also my perception and my truth.

What I have attempted to do through my inner search and understanding over the past recent years, is to no longer "conform" to anything or anyone. To no longer submit to the collective thought patterns and programming. To no longer submit to the status quo. But to claim back my own power by submitting instead to my personal inclinations and impulses. To do what comes naturally to me without undue influence of any kind. This new posture and outlook on life brought me closer to my Self. What a grand and beautiful discovery to simply be me. To sing my personal tune that has a resonance and consonance uniquely mine.

At long last, to be able to say naturally and effortlessly, I LOVE MYSELF.

CHAPTER ONE

Lost in a Maze

HEALING THROUGH MEDITATION AND DREAMS

When I first started meditating, about ten years ago, a lot of my unresolved inner conflicts came to the fore. Conflicts that I had not addressed and shoved, instead, into my subconscious mind. Through the years, as I continued meditating on a daily basis, I gradually became my own doctor, for I started to fully realize that every physical ailment had a psychosomatic origin. And if I was intent on healing myself, I had to seriously examine the nature of my emotions and feelings.

I remember after one particular meditation, the face of my gynecologist came forcefully to my mind and what he told me when I last saw him, approximately six years ago. I had asked him very specific questions, but he ignored most of them, and answered only one, hurriedly, concluding: "That's all you need to know."

I recall how very small and angry his answer made me feel, yet I said nothing and went home feeling belittled and unworthy.

That was one unpleasant day and I soon forgot about it. Consciously. Little did I know, then, that my subconscious mind had faithfully registered the emotions of that incident, and served them back to me a few years later with an anger greatly magnified, for I had dumped it and allowed it to fester within me.

Meditation has been, and continues to be, a powerful medicine acting as a catalyst that brings to the surface and helps me expel all the poison that I store within.

Meditation, as far as my personal experience goes, is a journey within the depth of Self. Before one could reach the core, the gold mine as it were, one has to go through many layers. The first ones have to do with cleansing, unresolved issues, before one can reach the next levels.

Initially, it was indeed very painful for me to look at myself, to look at my reactions. But it was necessary if I was to be serious about knowing my Self. The real Self that lay dormant beneath all the scraggy layers of frustrations, pent-up anger, self-hate, and rage that made me deaf and dumb, unaware of my potential buried deep under all those swarming and underlying emotional currents.

Those ignored emotions constituted an explosive and volatile Pandora's box that I had to learn to deactivate and neutralize.

So, as I started to meditate on a regular basis, all the issues in me that I hadn't addressed presented themselves one by one. I had to look at them, contemplate them, verbalize them and write them down. For it occurred to me that to know what I think and feel, I had to write it on paper. Otherwise, my thoughts remained in a nebula—scattered and incoherent like puffs of smoke.

Meditation has greatly helped me clear a lot of inner weeds and parasites; it has also shown me how to control my "monkey mind" otherwise known as the alter ego. Meditation has been for me a formidable cleanser that considerably enhanced my life over the past few years.

In addition to meditation, I have faithfully recorded my dreams, nearly every day, over the past twenty years or so. I am exceedingly glad I did, for reading some of them recently showed me clearly the pattern of my thought processes and the evolution of my consciousness through the years.

Some of my dreams were so farfetched and "unrealistic" that it took me years to understand their symbolism and meaning. But whatever I interpreted my dreams to be—hilarious, profound, nonsensical or meaningful—they greatly helped me discover an important aspect of myself, my subconscious mind.

Sometimes, there were dreams that I couldn't remember; however hard I strived to recall them, they completely eluded me. Upon waking all I could get was a fuzzy, hazy, vaporish feeling. Perhaps because those dreams had to do with another reality, another state of being—another dimension? Who knows? I had no reference point in my reality to measure, understand or grasp them. The only thing I had to go by was a feeling. Sometimes, it was a feeling of awe and wonder upon waking up, accompanied by a sense of exhilaration and freedom. And all I could say then was: WOW! Where did I just come from? I have to buy me a ticket to go back there. But where? The ticket counter was probably in a cloud somewhere.

Well, anyway, today I feel much lighter and more in control of my life. Looking at myself is no longer painful. On the contrary, it makes me laugh. I can look at my actions and reactions with a relative detachment and see the merit or comical aspect of them.

For truly life is a divine comedy.

A wonderful teacher of mine, Ramtha, kept repeating to me: "Life is not about pious misery. Life is pure joy." For a number of years those words were nothing more than wishful, fanciful thinking. Yet, at the same time, because I was determined to know myself, one day those words became my personal experience, my truth and my reality.

Everything stemmed from my own attitude. Whatever aspect of my life I didn't like, I changed it by changing my focus. All I had to do was to change my mind.

In retrospect, it appears so simple. It is. But because we have been heavily programmed by complexity, we do not look for answers in simplicity.

Over the past few years, through consistent meditation and focus on what I want to create in my personal reality, I have learned to get reacquainted with the child within me whose only aim is to discover and enjoy. To play and laugh. To learn and endlessly wonder why.

Chasing the word "WHY" as one would chase a butterfly. Playfully, joyfully, running and falling, crying and laughing, experiencing and living through the wild and wondrous field called life.

But, I am getting ahead of myself here. So, let's go back to my gynecologist who, by the way, triggered in me a whole chain of reactions and emotions that were a profound catalyst for my growth.

His attitude pushed my buttons to such an extent that it compelled me to focus on him for quite a while. The result was a retrospection of my life and an analysis of a society that we are both products of.

My gynecologist has indeed been instrumental in my inner growth, unbeknownst to him, and for that I shall always remain grateful to him.

For, whatever role anyone plays in our life, friend or foe, we derive from each a valid lesson and experience that strengthens our character and enlightens our nature.

Perhaps, the way to measure the quality of one's Spirit is to contemplate one's capacity of overcoming. How we weather the storm, ultimately, is how we can situate ourselves in life.

Weak or strong, the ball is in our own court.

A WORD OF ADVICE TO
MY GYNECOLOGIST

The last time I went to see my gynecologist for a medical check-up was about five years ago.

My doctor was talking to me about menopause—men-o-pause: the pause of men?—and somehow, intuitively, I felt that he was talking gibberish. Could it be that menopause, the pause of men, is a reprieve from men's subconscious knowledge of how very powerful women are? Possibly! Whoever invented that word knew what he was talking about.

Anyway, menopause is no part of my vocabulary or personal reality. I love everything about my womanhood. I have enjoyed thoroughly, without restriction, without inhibition, passionately, wholeheartedly every single aspect of it. The most beautiful aspect of my womanhood was bringing my two children into this world. Nurturing, loving my children, what a blessed experience it has been for me! To see them grow, play, laugh and challenge me, always challenging me with their wondrous questions and comments, as they were growing up—and me along with them.

So, I went to see my doctor one day, who by the way had told me over the years that I had the vital signs of a sixteen-year-old, not bad for a half centenarian! Anyway, he was telling me that soon my periods would be over and that I would be free of this "monthly nuisance."

Nuisance, the life force? Nuisance the vitality of my womanhood? Nuisance the core of creation in me? Nuisance, to give birth to the likes of you, doctor, so that you can show me how ignorant you are? You, whose job it is to maintain life, you were preparing me instead for death? Who taught you that, Doctor? Hippocrates? Was Hippocrates a hypocrite? He must have been!

Anyhow, doctor, I don't know very much about medical science, but enough to realize that every single cell in my body is there for a purpose. Every part of my cellular mass is there for a reason. The reason is to live. The only thing my consciousness is contemplating is vitality, energy and joy. The only thing I accept in my consciousness is life in all its aspects. My consciousness directs my cellular mass. And your merit, as a doctor, exists only insofar as I grant you that merit. Without it, your science becomes a powerless gobbledygook.

As you know, doctor, I have never been physically sick. I have always enjoyed great health throughout my life. Why? Because my womanhood, which is also endowed with a strong intuition, did not succumb to any programming about being careful of catching this disease or the other, or absorbing this tablet or the next. It was simply not part of my reality. In fact, I have never been careful about my health at all. Because I somehow felt that health was to forget about one's body, and let it tell one what it needs and when it needs it. My role was to respond accordingly. And not to tamper with it, as it is done by medical science, otherwise known as conventional medicine, preventive medicine. Preventing what? My awareness, that's for sure! So that you can implement your programming.

Yeah, prevention, convention, status quo, they have become abhorrent words to me lately. Which brings me to another subject. Alternative medicine. Some of your peers are actively involved in a merciless campaign against alternative medicine and the few wonderful naturopaths, as the name would suggest, who are more attuned to nature and the natural flow of the body. They help restore it, when need be, with natural elements, instead of dumping the whole pharmaceutical industry in it, like you are doing.

Ah, competition! The key word of this civilization, sadly involved in self-destruction. God help us all!

So, my dear doctor, I have nothing against you. All I am saying is adjust to the changes of time. Have you noticed lately how the conscious awareness of the public is on the rise? Things do not add up any longer and people are waking up to that fact. Amen to that! People no longer accept going to your office and being regarded as a piece of meat. Where your time is precious—ours is not?—and you are conducting five examinations simultaneously. And at what price!

So, here I was in your examination room for a routine check-up. Wasting my precious time and $200 to be poked, checked, manipulated, drained, pinched and punctured, to be finally told what I already knew perfectly: that I was in great health. And every year, I submitted to this charade in the name of preventive medicine. Not to mention that sometimes you sent me on a grand tour of the city to visit your colleagues. One specializing in X-Rays—isn't it kind of insane to shower my body with X-Ray radiations in the name of medical prevention? Especially as healthy a body as mine? Anyway, the other specializing in mammography, the next in cardiology, another in osteology—what a word! Why don't you just call it bones? Anyhow, I, a squeaky healthy woman, was sent to all your colleagues and by the time I was through with them, my monthly salary vanished in a puff of smoke; the smoke-screen of preventive medicine.

To make sure! said you. To make sure of what? That the mortgage payment of your second house was fully taken care of?

Your greatest skill, doctor, your greatest source of income, is your posture of intimidation. A wolf, in science clothing, preying on ignorant sheep. I recall in one of my visits to your office asking you specific questions and you answering me very vaguely and hurriedly, closing your statement by saying: "That's all you need to know."

Is that right? And who are you, doctor, to decide on the dosage of knowledge I am to receive?

You had also said that my uterus was retroverted. Rightfully so. Indeed, doctor, retroversion is the name of my game. I am looking back and reassessing everything. For I no longer accept this condescending, paternalistic and patronizing attitude you have towards your patients.

Anyway, coming back to my periods. Do you remember, doctor, about Sarah in the Bible? Sarah who gave birth to Isaac when she was ninety? Well, I have no plans, as I speak, of having any more children, but that doesn't mean that my reproductive system must not remain in perfect working order. And who knows? I may change my mind. Maybe fifty years from now, I may decide to have a baby. Wouldn't that be fun to defy the entrenched social belief claiming that a hundred-year-old woman cannot have children? Outrageous? Who says? The only limitations in life are those that I create. The only limitation I can see is to accept and make my truth the collective belief that says I can't. Everything is possible. If I can imagine it, I certainly can create it. There is no science in the world that can stand in the way of willpower. So, I definitely can, if my consciousness says so.

So, doctor, my reproductive system is the seat of creation. I want it as healthy as the rest of my body for as long as I live. I plan on living for a very long time, doctor. That's my will.

My reproductive system gives birth to humankind; men and women alike. I am, indeed, becoming fully aware of the divine powers bestowed on me by God, as a woman. By the way, God is male and female, yet neither. I trust you know that!

So, no male chauvinist, doctor or no doctor, is going to tell me about the status of my body and how I should handle it. Only I can decide that. Because my consciousness and my body are inextricably combined. They work in harmony with each other, in cooperation with each other. I am living proof of that.

You might find it worth your while to contemplate what I am telling you, doctor, as an ex-patient—patient, was I ever, for eons!—and start applying it with your own wife. Mercifully.

By the way, I hope you no longer subscribe to the preposterous notion that I am one of your ribs. Truth is, you are my child. A more likely story. History—his story—is not my story, it has been yours. Through my focused intent and determination to lift off the veils, I am attempting to rediscover my story and weed out all the lies it was buried under for eons. When I have acquired more knowledge about her story, I will narrate it as our story. Yours and mine. It will no longer be "history," it will become "Story." Authentic story, recorded and stored by both men and women. She, recording her contribution. He his own. That way, we will have the total picture. As it stands now, half of humanity is conspicuously missing from history. And how did the other half accomplish the deeds of history? You only neglected to mention the half that gave you birth, so that you could lie and falsify no end.

History, indeed! Speaking of which, I would like to share a little experience with you, doctor, that I had when I went to Nepal last year.

There, in the outskirts of Kathmandu, in a breathtaking environment, up on a hill overlooking the Himalayas far in the distance, there were fifty-five temples. Fifty-five. The central motif of worship in each temple was the lingam-yoni, the woman's genitalia representing the womb, in the center of which stood a male erected phallus. There was no lustful connotation about it whatsoever. On the contrary, I was in awe of it. I was in complete reverence of it. It stirred in me a strong and deep feeling of remembrance of my power that somehow got stamped out over the ages and made me a subservient, second-class citizen as a woman. Because what it meant was that the woman's womb—the void—was the seat from which all creation rises. You are one of that creation, as well as a participant, I must grant you that. My intention here is to be fair and to share equally with you everything that pertains to humankind's story. Its glory, as well as its shame.

By the way, doctor, fifty-five is a fascinating number. If we put these two fives face-to-face ?5 we have a wonderful container, the woman's womb; a beautiful bottle, the bottle of the Genie. The container of genius. Interestingly enough, the most beautiful artifacts in museums are vases, vessels, lovingly created by the potter, whose subconscious mind never made him forget his origins: the womb, the void. And so, the creation of the potter is the celebration of his home, his launching pad, his autobiography made manifest in a clay-pot. Blessed be he, blessed be she for remembering, in their creative adventure, the point of departure of their journey.

Now, if we add the number 55, we get 5 + 5 = 10, which is exactly the image of worship in those fifty-five temples. Let me explain what I understand the number 10 to mean:

1—the phallus. 1, the beginning of men's great adventure. 1, following zero to back it up.

0—the womb, the launching pad.

10—1 and 0 merged together, we have completion and unity of Self. The balance of male/female within.

It is so obvious, so beautifully simple! A wonderful teacher of mine, Ramtha, keeps repeating to me that one finds genius in simplicity. I am beginning to see more and more what he means. I have been illiterate far too long I suppose, unable to read what was around me.

So, my dear doctor, I want you to know that my ambitions are of an ever increasing nature. As a woman, I am waking up from my deep slumber. I am waking up from this long dream over which I had not much control: a dream in which my power and potential were suppressed and oppressed, covered-up and tampered with. Now that I am waking up, I can maneuver and direct, knowingly, my steps to the destination of my choice.

And so, my ambition being what it has become, it brings to mind a great Master of the Far East. Gautama Buddha. Ever heard of him? He was indeed a great master—master of his life and destiny—who ascended to heaven with his body. Yeah, some few thousand years ago, he put his consciousness to work and raised the energy level of his body to match his consciousness. And like a fiery rocket, off they both went to heaven.

Well, I am working on the same principle. And if on the day I ascend, I happen to have my periods, then I will ascend with a tampon. Glory be to womanhood! Glory be to humanhood!

* * * * *

I do not wish to conclude this talk, doctor, without trying to understand, come to terms with and reconcile what has been and why. Without attempting to go to the root of the problem and see what could be in the future.

I am very hopeful about the future, because perhaps some day soon, you will come to understand that by suppressing my power, you undermined yours. And that is truly a pity for both of us. But perhaps, you might say, it was an experience that had to be lived. The experience of imbalance. Well, for a while it served its purpose and did what it did, and here we both are, unhappy about the scale of things and the imbalances in the world, because they have snowballed over the millennia.

You had your field day, but I don't want to have mine at your expense. I want to start all over again, with you as an integral and fully equal partner.

The humanist in me is hopeful about the future. Our future,

doctor. So, by necessity, the truth is coming out of many closets. Conscientious objectors in all fields of endeavors are voicing their grievances and denouncing the abuses of the institutions they represented. It can no longer be stopped. It can no longer be stifled. The cat is out of the bag. One cat after another, rolling in waves upon waves of collective awareness. Indeed, "the truth shall set us free."

Right now, I am looking, I am observing, I am learning. I am wondering. I can't help it.

You know something, doctor, each time I went to see you, I was saddened by your attitude and posture. I still am. I can't help wondering what happened to you as you entered into the medical field and progressed—or rather regressed—in it. In my heart, I know, you decided to become a medical doctor to serve and to heal. From this lofty and high ideal, you descended, gradually, into the murky and troubled waters of money and power. Of competition and social recognition.

What happened to that lofty concept? What happened to that inspiring ideal? Did you ever ask yourself, doctor, why that ideal transmuted into a sour reality? Maybe, over the years, that ideal slipped away and got trapped. It became entangled in the "should" and "must" of social programming. Maybe, you immersed yourself in it. Or maybe you simply misinterpreted one of the tenets of the Hippocratic oath and applied it literally : "...being honored with fame among all men for all time to come..."

You lost sight, doctor, of the bigger picture. The decision you originally made, in humility, to serve, somehow degenerated into weakness. Falling prey to the alter ego's need for power and control over others.

You view your patients as an anonymous flock. Each of them, nothing more than "a piece of meat" to mend. Your compassion for them disappeared along the way. Oh sure, you may have eased the physical pain, but the soul remained deeply wounded. And that is what needs to be healed, doctor. For the soul yearns for kindness and understanding. It yearns for gentleness and mercy. Most of all, it yearns for justice.

Those qualities, doctor, exist in everyone of us, without exception. The only difference is that in some of us they are in a frozen state and in some others they flow, naturally.

What we need to do, doctor, is to thaw out those qualities. Do you remember when you first took your Hippocratic oath? What a beautiful day it must have been! Intuitively, I can just picture you in that moment. I can feel your emotions, then, shining through. The emotions of a beautiful humanitarian spirit. Taking your Hippocratic oath, you said among other things: "...I will keep the sick from harm and injustice... In purity and holiness, I will guard my life and my art..."

I would like to have given you a heartfelt hug on that day, doctor. Unfortunately, today's reality is a far cry from that moment.

Purity and holiness of thoughts and deeds, is what we all have to come back to. To stop and reflect, for a moment, on how profoundly each of us affects the other, and the endless ramifications of our thoughts and deeds in all our interactions. It is time for us to lay to rest thoughtlessness and manipulation, and start to become more mindful of what we do to each other. This change of attitude is our only hope for salvation, doctor.

Coming back to the social fabric, I am putting two and two together. All this incredible tapestry called "social structure" doesn't add up any longer. What an entangled web! What a formidable trap! Propaganda everywhere! Science —the religion of the 20th century—accepts only facts, the tangible and the concretely demonstrable, and becomes entangled in its steel and stone rigidity. Where did the tangible come from, doctor? The Spirit that presides over it. God forbids that the Spirit be part of any scientific book! And so, without Spirit, it goes on its merry blind way.

Economics, politics, religion, mass media, medical science, industries, all these institutions are working hand in hand together. All these institutions determine the quality of air I am to breathe, the kind of thoughts I am supposed to think, the preventive measures I am to take, what products I am to acquire, the kind of life I am to lead, making sure that I take into account all of them and dare not venture outside of the beaten path traced by all this programming. Constantly prying on my weakness.

And I, stifled, muffled, intimidated, intimated and persuaded, I complied, danced and dangled, like a puppet, for eons.

Don't you find it an incredible miracle that I still exist? Human resilience is, indeed, something I greatly marvel at.

But this puppet is breaking loose. This puppet has cut off the strings of the status quo. That's it. I cannot be dangled around any longer. I am taking charge. I am taking full charge of my life.

I am shutting off the programming. I no longer read the newspapers. I no longer watch television. The time I wasted on both of them I now use to meditate and focus on what is relevant to my life. I am doing my own thinking by allowing the subtle voice within me to emerge. I am giving full reign to it. It is my wisest counsel. It gives me all the remedies I happen to need at any given moment.

To hear it properly, I go within. I close my eyes and center myself. In stillness and silence, I am gradually learning to get in touch with myself. I have a greater sense of direction because of that.

Yes doctor, I am taking charge of my health, my happiness, what to think and what to do. No one can provide any of that for me except my consciousness. I am creating my own reality and having a ball in the process.

I have never been so joyful in my life. Joy, doctor, is contagious. I plan to express it and spread it around. My friendly suggestion to you is that you start also to reassess everything before you are out of a job. What are you going to do, doctor, when there are only joyful people around?

Perhaps it is time for you to contemplate another career. Won't that be fun? What do you dream about, doctor? What is your hobby? Perhaps that's where your next career lies. Glory be to change! And perhaps it will be your turn, then, to tell the pharmaceutical industry to reassess everything. Some kind of a possible domino effect. A wonderful domino effect.

Because, you see, doctor, lately I have also felt this surge of love, this great compassion in the face of so much pain, so much sadness and torment. You know something, when I see an individual in the street who seems so very sad and lost, so bewildered, I want to give him a hug and words of comfort. But I don't do that because I don't want to scare him off. The programming in us is so thick that we are afraid of each other; of everyone. We can't recognize one another any longer. Why is that, doctor?

Aren't you, like me, tired of all this pain and suffering? Tablets and pills, doctor, are not the cure. Slicing up the flesh with the scalpel is even worse. The cure, doctor, is mercy. Mercy for one another. The cure is stopping the lies, the manipulation, the use, the abuse, the games, the holier-than-thou-posture. The cure, doctor, is to look at one another for the first time and see a self-reflection.

We have to heal doctor, individually and collectively. It is imperative. It is urgent. It is a matter of life or death.

I plan on living, doctor. What about you?

Why are we at odds with each other? Why can't you find gratification without having power over me? Over anyone? Why is there this formidable need to control others, this unquenchable lust for power?

Is it the depth of the dizzying hollowness inside, doctor, that explains it? Is it the cerebral fissure that is the cause? Why don't you, like me, try to go within and uproot this sense of loss within? Instead of making do, making shift and covering it up with holding on to power. That hollowness inside won't go away unless you do something about it and address it. When you do, you will bridge the gap and, one day, you might feel whole again. This is what I am trying to do, my dear doctor.

And when that gap is bridged, you will do away with the pharmaceutical industry. After all, industrialists are human beings too. Bless our hearts all. World peace starts with individual peace. My personal contribution to world peace, doctor, is making peace with myself.

Yes, doctor, programming and propaganda are wearing thin. The only thing that varies from one society to the next on this planet is the degree and subtlety in which that propaganda is delivered. From one society to the next, fear and guilt are administered either crudely or subtly. The more subtle it is, the more insidious the programming; the more insidious, the more subliminal it becomes; the more subliminal, the more volatile, like ether, difficult to fully trace. It escapes one's understanding.

I must acknowledge here the extraordinary cleverness and far-reaching insight of the oligarchs who conceived, designed and implemented such mega control world-wide.

So, this subtle programming is more prevalent in western societies. In the rest of the world it is plainer, it is administered more crudely. At least one knows where one stands there.

As I was saying, this programming in the West is more subtle. But without fear, government would not exist. Without guilt, religion would not exist.

And what kind of a society would we have without government or religion? A happy society, doctor. A sane society. For, having done away with the neurosis of fear and guilt inoculated by the controlling institutions, freed from the grip of these two tormentors, the individual would realize, for the first time, that there is more to life than mere survival, struggle, suspicion, fear—ever-increasing fear—and guilt, always guilt and the sinking feeling it triggers inside. The helplessness and paralysis that fear and guilt create. A helpless and paralytic society, it is quite clear, can be controlled effortlessly.

Some of us, doctor, have a more fragile psychological make-up than others. Some of us have more difficulty than others to absorb and digest, to inhale and breathe the pollution of all this programming.

People who are in hospitals, people who are in jails, people who are in mental institutions, doctor, bless their souls, bless them all, can't take it any more. They suffer from an overdose of programming. And so, they lost their balance. Poor souls, they became trapped further in the pains of their minds and bodies. The pressure became too intense, the hollowness inside too acute, and the intensity created shock waves in their thought processes.

Confused thinking leads to confused action. Painful thinking leads to physical pain, to mental pain, to physical disease.

And so, hospitals, jails and asylums are filled to the brim. And what happens to all these poor individuals? In hospitals, they are being poked, sliced up, punctured and anesthetized to numb the pain, to numb the awareness.

In jails, they are treated crudely, rudely, unmercifully. And this lack of respect, this lack of charity for basic human decency, flares up as more unrest, more violence, which leads to more vicious punishment. What a wretched vicious circle!

In asylums they are showered with more electrical shocks, tranquilized and pacified into walking vegetables. Walking dead with less and less ability to understand, to appreciate and to enjoy. Their spirit has been knocked out, senseless.

And the people who take care of all of the above? Bless their souls too for their hard work and resilience. All the doctors and nurses, administrators and administrative assistants. All the wardens and workers—they are stressed out as well and trapped in their own jobs. But what can they do? They have families to feed at home, bills and mortgages to pay, payments to insurance companies to cover their small and big assets; lawyers' fees to protect their deeds and assets. To protect what they do not own because of mortgage payments and insurance policies.

Society's intricate web, when one sees the whole tapestry, is truly a formidable hoax. It would appear as a hilarious joke if it were not played with such deadly seriousness.

Is that what life is all about? Paying bills to survive? That's it?

Bills, bills. Bills to pay the lawyers. Lawyers, preying on all these weak points, seizing the opportunities of all these loopholes; some of them licking their whiskers at the prospect of the chunks of money to be had—the chunks of money they are going to gobble up their client with. Bless their souls as well. They too became entangled in the programming; they too are the victims of it. Their brand of psychology is of a different kind. It is not that of hot heads like the so-called misfits of society. Their brand of psychology is colder, more calculating. Their personal absorption of the programming is total implementation of the programming. Their heart got numb too. It became a little colder from one decade to the next, a little greedier from one era to the next.

A few years ago, a lawyer charged me $500 to avoid paying a fine of $500. And, like an intimidated idiot, I paid it. That's how smart I was.

So, as I was saying, the lawyers got a little more stiff, a little more rigid, and oh, so very, very, cynical. God, have mercy on us all!

The lawyers lost themselves in their own game. But I understand, doctor, I feel the pain of their coldness. In their great oratorical pontifications, they drown their feelings in the cold waters of their hearts. I understand. They too have to make a living, they have a standing, a reputation in society to uphold. They channel their personal pressure into an ever vicious competitiveness, to make an overkill—literally and figuratively. Indeed, they have to uphold their own reputation. Society demands it. A reputation of wealth, a standard of living to show for it. And, rigidly, in cooperation with the police force, they implement the rules and regulations, ever increasing, ever stifling rules and regulations.

What a formidable trap! What a machiavellian social structure!

Why, dear God, why? For the gratification of those who designed this social structure? Those who, at the apex of the pyramid of society, created this world order. This world chaos. Bless their hearts as well. Their unquenchable lust for power, their dizzying need to control—to control us all—their bewildering design to have dominion over our thoughts and actions, their disease is the most poignant of all.

Because, once they control us all, totally, then what? Their peculiar sense of joy, derived from this collective subjugation and suffering, how long can it be sustained? How long until their tormented and twisted minds that compel them to control at any cost, to exercise power at all cost, how long until their chilling hearts have had their fill of the uniform greyishness they created? The uniform gloom they created globally?

For their ultimate goal, it is clear, is not money. Money is only the means to their goal. Their goal is to have ultimate power, ultimate control over us.

41

Power for power's sake.

How many of the controllers are there? Probably a handful. Maybe fifty. Maybe a hundred.

My dear doctor, I am trying to understand here. To think that a handful of people can have dominion over nearly six billion of us! How could that be? This truly defies all basic common sense. Is there any of it left anywhere?

We have bought and fallen prey to the social programming designed by them to such a degree that our weakness and lack of willpower—our lethargy and complacency—our incredible submissiveness as flocks marching, willingly, to the slaughter house of power, gave them an ever increasing boldness to take advantage of the situation and turn us all into walking dead.

That's how and why the oligarchs—those tyrants—could design such a formidable social trap. But, what if each of us were to wake up? What if each of us were to come alive again and break loose from the shackles of all this programming? Do you think they would have a fighting, flipping chance? I would think not!

We would put them into an imposed retreat. But we wouldn't give them any pills or electrical shocks, for then we wouldn't have understood anything. No. We would confine them in beautiful surroundings, in a very large real estate, where the only mirrors they would have would be a variety of plants, flowers and beautiful rocks and stones. A plethora of trees and birds of all kinds. And across that estate, throughout, water falls, running meadows and babbling brooks soothing to the soul, and everywhere, birds singing their hearty and melodious songs.

Birds, oblivious to human behavior and mercifully singing the song of life to them. Perhaps those songs would trigger feelings in their souls; they would make the tyrants' hearts sensitive again to the beauty and harmony of nature. To the nature of humans to have the right to be part of that natural harmony, instead of raping it for profit and power.

And the meadows would softly whisper to the oligarchs an understanding: the understanding that the natural flow of life cannot be stopped, it can only evolve. For, in the spectrum of life's probabilities and outcome, they chose to experience power and tyranny. And that too is a valid lesson for humanity to learn and benefit from. They are enacting that particular game and living that dream. That is their contribution to humanity. Displaying the dark side of genius.

Because of that, because of them, humanity is experiencing and learning another aspect of human behavior. In the grand scheme of things, beyond narrow and petty considerations, beyond subjectivity and anger, indeed, in a greater understanding, the likes of Hitler and Mother Teresa are equally valid, equally meaningful. One highlights the other. A definite learning in contrast and opposite.

Yes, that's the understanding the soft meadows and the babbling brook would convey to them. And who knows, maybe they would be able to hear and decipher the language of the flowing waters.

So, in such an environment and without computers, without telephone, without any electronic device of any kind—electronic devices, the vice and plague of the 20th century—we would put, instead, books in their hands. Not telefaxes, but facts. Books to read, when and if they felt like reading. For they would not be coerced to do anything. Books written by those who object to oligarchy. Conscientious objectors who oppose tyranny and wonder why there is so much pain and suffering, and what for? To whose benefit?

Those books would mirror back to this handful of oligarchs that presiding over a society of victims could not be sustainable indefinitely. That increasing the notch of destruction of our minds, our bodies and our planet cannot go on ad eternam, without society completely destroying itself and the tyrants tumbling down with it. For, when society is completely destroyed, who are the oligarchs going to have power over? Empty streets and cities?

I am trying to understand and put myself in the tyrants' shoes. How challenging could it possibly be to constantly lead and interact with victims? It seems to me far more inspiring and enlightening to interact with equals and superiors, in terms of insight and intelligence. Because then it makes one expand, grow and stretch. But, for them to constantly interact with victims could only be constricting and retracting.

Even if the victims are great geniuses and great minds, those qualities could not expand to their full measure because of the degree of control and fear in them. Fear of being victimized further, fear of revealing to the oligarchs too much knowledge that could be used against them and against humanity.

It is said that "the greatest of things are achieved with a light heart." So, with a heart heavy with fear, one can only achieve the least of things. The approximate, not the ultimate. No wonder science, today, has become reactionary and dares not to even consider, let alone integrate, the possibility that truth and reality can be found elsewhere than in the tangible, the demonstrable, the concrete, objective world. No wonder they have a fragmented understanding of reality.

And yet, their statements and conclusions have become words of an Evangelist. The final word in a world mesmerized by the scientific community that seems to overlook the facts of its own history, where from one era to the next, one century to the next, there emerged one scientist who completely refuted the established theory. One scientist who changed and evolved science from its entrenched posture of the day.

What would it take for them to consider that there is far more to the material world than meets the eye in any laboratory. That what the microscope and the telescope reveal are only a fragment of reality, a fragment of the truth. Not all of it.

That's why we must wake up and put the oligarchs in a retreat. To think things over. To cool off. To recover from their disease for power and control. To start to reverse the process in them and begin the journey from constriction to expansion. Not expansion at our expense. Expansion for our mutual benefit. They too are our mirrors. Our escape from lethargy and submissiveness will help purge them of their tyranny and fantasy for total control.

Yes, doctor, this is my reasoning today.

Utopia, all of this? Indeed. All utopias are possible, doctor. All utopias can be made manifest with consistent focus and determination. The peculiar utopia of the oligarchs is quite clear for everyone to see. Their focus and willpower was unwavering for a very, very long time. And here it is, doctor. They have gone very far with it. They are very close to absolute control.

EVERYTHING IS POSSIBLE. The tyrants are an absolute proof of that. Indeed, doctor, once one is open to the fact that anything is possible, the impossible, in time, will become common occurrence.

And whatever you deem or perceive me to be—crazier than the lot—I am, doctor, a voice crying in the wilderness. The wilderness being plundered, raped, slashed, levelled to the ground and transformed into barren and sterile condominiums.

A voice in the silenced humanity. Humanity turned into, and walking like, an anonymous flock of zombies. Humanity silenced by the programming, and marching like controlled robots.

I am a voice in the wilderness of closed minds, echoing and hoping that, somehow, this echo would not fall only on deaf ears, but on yours, doctor.

Please hear me out.

The controlling institutions would not, could not possibly exist without fear and guilt. The origin of our aching body is guilt and fear. It is more than a wound we have inside, doctor, it is a crater. To go across that crater, and eventually one day completely close that gap, what we need is a formidable bridge. We are all endowed with that bridge, doctor, it is called willpower. All we have to do is pull it out of its deep slumber.

And when we have closed and healed that gap inside, we will be whole again. We will develop the joy of living, the joy of being. For you see, doctor, a joyful individual hates no one, a joyful individual feels no guilt and has no fear. A joyful individual is innately moral, knows innately the right thing to do and is endowed with respect for others, because he/she has self-respect.

So, if one is innately moral, why does one need rules and regulations that strap the individual in a straitjacket? Why does one have need for the electrical shocks given by propaganda on the poor soul who reacts with a sense of disorientation, loss, depression and cannot make heads or tails of anything in his life? Running, helpless, towards the very institutions that created the trauma in the first place. And so, he is drugged a little more by the doctor and turned into a vegetable by the mesmerizing images of the television.

Television, the deadliest of all drugs. Television where the two most important mediums of entertainment are violence and sex. Television, where day time soap operas are the most formidable marketing trap, cleverly devised to manipulate the televiewer into a frantic consumer.

SOAP OPERAS. They are, indeed, a manipulative force for all televiewers to see, if they bother to look. Turning us, subliminally, into compulsive consumers. The dramas that unfold in those soap operas, from one day to the next, are manifold in terms of the programmer's aim. The programmer's aim, first and foremost, is marketing. To keep the public focused only on the material aspect of life. It is also to maintain a perpetual sense of drama and conflict, in the televiewer's mind, keeping him/her constantly entertained and less and less in touch with Self. Constantly suggesting that there is nothing more to life than drama, conflict, greed, mistrust and manipulation in every conceivable way possible.

So, in the setting of any particular soap opera, what is displayed masterfully is the home in which the actors perform. In most instances, it is a rich and elegant home, filled with beautiful and antique furniture, lavishly displayed. Giving a subliminal idea to the viewer on how to decorate his/her home. To lust after a piece of furniture or two, a particular carpet, or a garden landscaping; dreaming about that Jaguar or Cadillac in the garage. Immersing the viewers in a daydream of material wealth and comfort. Triggering in their minds a desire to aspire, strive and reach, at all cost, the standard of living being displayed on the TV screen.

The programmer, cleverly, overlooks the fact that the viewers are from all walks of life. Whereas the performing actors portray, almost exclusively, the so-called upper crust of society. Namely doctors, lawyers, judges, politicians, publishers, heads of big corporations, fashion designers, and the likes.

This creates, in the viewer's mind, who is none of the above, and whose income is nowhere near what he/she sees on those shows, a great difficulty to identify with and relate to what he sees; a sense of inadequacy. A lack of self-esteem for failing to have such a lifestyle.

"THE LIFESTYLE OF THE RICH AND THE FAMOUS"

Triggering conflicting feelings in the viewer's heart. Feelings of admiration, mixed with envy, jealousy and inadequacy all at once. All this display of wealth is supposed to be an ideal to which everyone should aspire to. To dream big.

Is that all a dream is? Is that the extent of the collective aspirations? A house full of furniture? That's it?

That part of the programming—which is also deliberately devised—triggers some kind of chain reaction and neurosis. Hence, headaches and physical discomforts that warrant all kinds of commercials for tablets and pills to cure them.

Also, every season, the actors wear the latest fashion. Suggesting what's "in" and what to buy in terms of clothing in any given season.

And what about the scripts? Well, they instill in the viewer's mind an addiction to drama and conflict. A sense of wicked joy derived from watching other people's sorrows. Reinforcing a judgmental attitude as well as a gratifying need for indignation. It keeps the viewers out of touch with themselves and perpetually focused on the world out there, never within.

The dramas also maintain that life is a tragedy, full of pain, suffering, difficulties and wickedness. A very destructive programming subliminally, but very much in line with the programmer's intentions.

Life is not tragic, doctor. It is pure joy. How does one experience joy? By a change of attitude, by a radical change of focus.

Everything returns to its point of origin. The thoughts that one expels and projects from one's mind go to the universe in order to find situations that exactly match their nature. Subsequently, those thoughts return to one as tangible reality and experiences.

To expect the worst, to view on the TV screen the worst scenarios day in, day out, year after year, one can only magnetize the worst. If one projects negative expectations, one cannot very well harvest positive situations.

So, those soap operas are also signifying to the public, in no uncertain terms, that doctors, lawyers, judges, etc., have miserable times also; that they, too, experience great pains and difficulties. Suggesting to the viewer to accept his/her lot in life and not to complain too much. To just continue to work hard and consume even harder. It doesn't matter if one has money or not. Just charge it. Television turning the public into a frantically consuming society which doesn't own most of what it has: car, house, furniture, even television. It's all a grand display of everyone's debts. A pathetic parade where everyone, everywhere, is trying to keep up with the "Joneses."

And you may argue, doctor, that some people own their home. That's an illusion. For even if the last mortgage premium is made on a house, one still has to pay taxes on it every year, as well as an insurance policy. If one fails to do so, one may lose it. The same goes for one's car. So, no one ever owns anything. The tax system makes sure of that.

But, that's another story. I won't get into it right now. For, the endless and intricate ramifications of social programming are of such complexity, of such a magnitude of entrapment, that it will take me volumes to cover it all.

So, doctor, coming back to soap operas. The conflicting signals of such programming create in the viewer's mind some difficulty to assimilate the contradictions of TV images and messages. On the one hand it suggests becoming materially wealthy; on the other, it is saying that material wealth doesn't bring happiness.

VIOLENCE. The more violent the TV plot, the more gory the details day in, day out. Over the years, the mind slides into numbness as horror becomes common place and boring. And the adrenaline pumping in the programmer's blood stream to keep the TV ratings up; frantically devising ever increasing horrors to keep the televiewer interested. A kind of opium and poison to keep the intoxication going, all around, in everyone's mind. Everywhere.

Whatever happened to wholesomeness and simple ways of living? Whatever happened to simple joys and decency? They have become laughable matters. The rare characters on TV who portray those qualities are made fun of and considered "simpletons" and ignorant. And what are they ignorant about? Complexity and cynicism. They do not know how to be cynical.

They are beautifully simple. Simplicity, in today's society, makes no sense, for the social and mental fabric is complexity. And so, simplicity has become contemptible.

SEX. The beauty of the sexual act, where two human beings embrace one another, is exposed on TV. The beauty and sacredness of that act is being degraded, defamed and profaned. The beauty of that act, which should be as private and personal as one's heart and imagination, is displayed crudely. And so, the sexual act is no longer a spontaneous development of two individuals desiring to know each other, but a mechanical and mindless act to be viewed, evaluated and judged by others. Millions of others.

The sacredness and poetry of sexual intercourse, the extraordinary mystery of love-making, have all vanished. Instead, what we have are talk shows telling us how to do it. On radio waves, in magazines, on TV. Everywhere. And so, the insidiousness of the programming has intruded into the most private of places—one's bedroom. And all these talk shows could succeed in doing is further increase the collective confusion. For what is relevant to one, may not be to the other. How could one conform to, and identify with, the collective programming where sexuality is concerned? Where every shred of spontaneity has been tampered with. And what is left? Nothing. Its essence and beauty have been stripped bare. What is left is an animal act. At least animals do not have contempt for each other while doing it. To them, it is not a fight for power. It is a natural process.

What a pity, my dear doctor. What a pathetic situation. It makes one want to weep and weep at what we have become as a human species. For, anyone who buys pornographic magazines, anyone who watches violent TV shows, endorses those programs and accepts their messages. The messages of abuse and degradation of the human spirit and body. The degradation of Self.

What is wrong with us, doctor, that we belittle ourselves to such a degree? What is wrong with us that we inflict so much pain on our body and soul? Why have we arrived at such formidable self-hatred?

Is it any wonder that we have been stripped of our freedom? That all we are fed is more garbage, generating more self-hatred? Where does all this stop? Where does all this end? When do we wake up and say, "Enough!"?

Coming back to joy, doctor—a joyful individual is someone who is in alignment with his soul. An individual experiencing the "kingdom of heaven." And where is that? "Surely not in a piece of real-estate somewhere in the sky" would comment Ramtha; the kingdom of heaven is within. Within are all the answers and solutions.

The last frontier, doctor, is WITHIN. And the day one realizes that, one no longer has a need to resort to artifices or torment one's body with drugs, alcohol and debauchery.

Debauchery is the unfortunate consequence of pornography prevalent everywhere and brought about by the mass media without inhibition. Without any consideration. The only thing considered is profit.

Yes, doctor, the day one decides to go within, one starts to get in touch with self and does away, gradually, with programming of any kind. Does away with escaping and becomes centered again. In alignment with Self.

Next time you look at yourself in the mirror, doctor, before shaving, ask yourself who is hiding behind the pair of eyes facing you? Who is holding that cellular mass of yours together? Your beautiful, your awesome spirit. The God within you, who wants you to have it all. Effortlessly, guiltlessly, fearlessly.

The extraordinary spirit within you, whose subtle voice you have stifled with the noise of your daily activities of must and should; of achievement and competition; of standing and standard of living.

Because, if in your daily life, all that you witness is pain and suffering, degradation and tragedy, you haven't achieved very much. Have you?

How often, doctor, did you think over your diagnostics to the poor women whom you have recommended a hysterectomy? Mutilating her in the very essence of her gender, of her womanhood? In all the bulk of your thick and heavy medical books, was there no information, no indication, no alternative, to prevent such a drastic measure?

A true sign of evolution, doctor, is for you to have fewer and fewer patients, because you truly know how to heal. But if your patients keep coming back, their helplessness attached to a great need for you and your own needs attached to your power over them, and over their wallet, what have you accomplished, doctor?

You have acquired more material goods and a thicker wallet, but are you happy with that? Are you peaceful inside? No, sometimes you get very sick. As much as your patients, you are also prone to cancer, AIDS and every malady imaginable.

And that is something that has always baffled me. A medical doctor who is ill physically. How could you be sick, and a healer? This formidable knowledge that you have, you spent at least ten years acquiring it in a medical school. Knowledge of physics, chemistry, biology, anatomy. What good is it, to what avail, if you, as a doctor, are susceptible to those diseases? With your knowledge of preventive medicine, how come you couldn't prevent anything where you are concerned? Then, by my book, you are not a doctor at all. Only one eye blind, leading astray a flock of totally blind people, your patients.

Your services are those of a healer. You are selling health. What credibility could you possibly have if you are diseased?

How could I buy your services if you are not a perfect example of what you are selling? Could it be that the answer to health, for patients and doctors alike, is not in medical books, but in consciousness? In one's attitude? In one's outlook on life?

Perhaps, doctor, it is time for you to recognize, in humility, that you do not have all the answers, that you are as vulnerable as the rest of us.

Perhaps it is time for you to listen more attentively and compassionately to what your patients are telling you. It is time for you to slow down and give each patient the attention she deserves. Because without your patients, you are nowhere as a doctor.

If my opinion sounds a little harsh to you, it is because my personal experience with the medical field has been harsh to me. Look at us, doctor, with understanding. Take the time to listen to what we are telling you, verbally and silently.

Your patients, doctor, are your source of income. Do not have contempt any longer for the hands that feed you. For, if they do not have much knowledge of medical science, they certainly have expertise in their own field of endeavor. A subject you probably know nothing about. They work hard and endure. How else could they come up with the outrageous sums of money you require of them? They endure a great deal, indeed. And that, in itself, deserves much respect.

You know something else, doctor? One could make a parallel

between the two halves of humanity—men and women—and the two halves of the brain, the left and right hemispheres.

The right hemisphere deals with emotions and intuition: women. The left hemisphere deals with reason and action: men. Both are vitally important.

If one looks through the haze and maze of human history, one can more or less trace how men and women became divided. How the struggle for power and survival started. Creating havoc in human behavior. Creating a painful dichotomy in humanity.

Does the answer lie in the brain? Why isn't the brain whole? Why is there a longitudinal cerebral fissure dividing the two hemispheres? How did the brain get divided into two parts? Does your science say anything about that?

I am very curious about the subject, doctor. It might be worth your while to find out the cause, instead of only tackling the effect—as medical science does—therefore never really solving anything.

All we do is keep turning in circles: superficially mending the surface and leaving intact the root of the problem. Just spinning our wheels endlessly and blindly.

There is an origin and a cause to everything. That's where we have to look, doctor. We have to go beyond appearances and learn to see, perhaps for the first time, not with our temporal eyes, but with an inward vision, an inward understanding.

Explore other avenues of research, research that doesn't have to do with laboratory tools of steel and chrome, but the impalpable. The human psyche. The only tools necessary for that are stillness and silence. Silence the uproar around and within, and listen to the answers emerging from one's being. For, the material world is a projection of the inner world, the spiritual world, and not the other way around. The day science finally accepts that, we can all heave a sigh of relief; we would, then, all have made a great leap forward.

The examination of dead bodies, doctor, dissecting and fragmenting them, just increases the mystery. It cannot reveal very much about the functions of an alive body. The perfect functions of the total body.

To know and discover more about a living human body, one has only to still one's body and mind into silence, meditation and contemplation and, as patiently as in laboratory research, wait, observe and feel one's mind and body under such a process.

The day everyone does this and shares their inner explorations and findings to enlighten one another, science will have become a tool to the benefit of humanity and nature, everywhere. The life of guinea pigs would, then, mercifully, be spared to allow life, everywhere, to flourish.

You have chosen a very challenging profession, doctor. A very ambitious one. Gynecologist. Wow!

Tell me, doctor, what do you know about carrying a child within you for nine months? What do you know about childbirth pains? About daily child rearing and emotions? As far as I know, you haven't given birth to a child, or stayed at home with that child, day in, day out; year in, year out, to raise it? Sure, you have your theories on the subject, but what are they? One only knows what one experiences, physically and emotionally. And clearly, this is not your case.

This job, it seems to me, is more befitting to a woman. Unfortunately, because of programming, many female gynecologists have adopted the male posture. Aloof, distant, inaccessible and quite haughty.

Yes, some women have become very good at monkeying and copying your attitude, and sadly lost their originality in the process. To be accepted by you, to survive and evolve on your turf, she had to flatter you, by imitating you. And that's how the natural softness and gentleness of women got lost in the process. The graceful feminine touch, the appealing feminine quality and appearance became a "no no" to many professional women. How unfortunate! How very sad that many women should lose their beautiful femininity because of their decision to call the shots in their life; because of their decision to empower themselves by realizing and bringing to life their own potential. Then they haven't achieved much either. And if, in order to gain power, she has to lose her happiness because the male gender feels threatened by that power, then both men and women are in a sorrowful situation, indeed.

In my book, self-empowerment means having control over my life. Because I do, I respect the same need in everyone else. Self-respect begets respect for others. And who says that power and femininity don't go together? Perhaps both men and women should redefine what that term means. How very sad it is to observe, sometimes, many so-called "professional" women exhibiting a haughty attitude towards those who decided to stay at home, thereby adopting the same male condescending attitude. Does her social status make her wiser than her counterpart who stays at home? Well, I let you be the judge of that, doctor.

As for the women, in general, who compete with one another for your affection and attention—well, I won't get into that snake pit right now. Their hostility for one another is the most sorrowful and poignant of all, because they have been programmed, for eons, to derive their sense of worth, their financial, and emotional support from you.

So, that's what we have become, doctor. A very neurotic society. A neurotic species, that got entangled in the programming and acted against our nature, against our better judgement and natural inclination, to conform to the programming. Losing ourselves in the programming.

Homosapiens. Homo-sap-iens. The sap of the homo running haywire. A sense of loss and dizziness, an emotional hollowness triggering wars, diseases, intolerance, racism, bigotry, and unrest everywhere. Scattering and fragmenting our collective energy, and channeling it into a formidable hostility towards others. The only thing that prevails is a defensive posture ready for the offensive at any moment.

The thunderous uproar of humanity, the discordant cacophony of its contradictory system of values has made us deaf and blind, seriously damaging our perception and vision.

Cause and effect. The origin of any situation. That's what we have to look at, seriously, if we are to recover from our present blindness.

What fascinates me, right now, is the word "gynecology".

Gyn-eco: echo of genes? Logy: logic?

Gynecology: the logic of genes?

Could it be that the genesis of logic comes from women? A simple speculation on my part. But anyway, how do we—you and I—become a homo - gene - ous whole? Homogeneous. How can you and I become a coherent unity?

Homogeneous, indeed.

Homo-genius, probably.

Genius. The gen - in - us.

Any way I look at it, I have the word "Gene." The isness of genes. The genesis, the genes - is - ness of life. And how these genes are handled and manipulated, how the game is played, is what gives us the outcome.

And here we are.

As I was saying, doctor, when an individual has achieved peace of mind, regardless of the uproar that surrounds him, he respects his body thoroughly and realizes also that his body houses a living God. What need is there, after that, for religion? For I am, doctor, indeed as you are, a divine spark. And as such, in the likeness of God, I create and design my life, in whatever way I chose. That's called free will, I believe. And I fully intend to exercise it without any undue influence of any kind.

It just occurred to me, right now, that it is kind of reassuring to know that I can voice my grievances, today, without worrying about being burned at the stake, like in the Middle Ages. Where my present utterings would have been considered as those of a witch or a heretic.

At least, that's some progress! Though, I realize, that today's burning at the stake is of a different nature. It is called ridicule, I believe.

No matter, in the process of coming to terms with and understanding myself, this reassessment of mine, this prospect and retrospect, were necessary. One has to nip things in the bud; one has to go back to the cause and origin of things. It was imperative for me to verbalize what weighed heavily on my psyche in order to transcend it all and arrive at a place of detachment and understanding. Understanding comes about, doctor, when one attempts to look at the whole picture.

Yes, doctor, the idealist that I am is contemplating a day when, at long last, we will recognize and salute one another for who we are, individually, uniquely. We will create and expand collectively, inspiring one another by our respective endeavors, by our respective explorations, by our respective creations.

The truth shall set me free. Indeed, doctor, for me the veil is off. I am being healed from my blindness. I no longer walk in the dark, recognizing nothing and no one. I can see better now. Indeed, doctor, freedom is my aim and destination. Freedom from the bondage of social programming; freedom from the constraints of "should" and "must."

"Should" and "must" served a purpose for a while. I experienced them fully. Now I am leaving them behind. It is time to move on, for I have paid long enough and fully, my dues of submission and boredom.

Indeed, I see better now, doctor. And if the glare of all this truth is somewhat painful, at least it doesn't make me wobbly any longer. My footing is on a safer ground. My safety is my faith, for my consciousness has firmed it up, and stabilized it into a greater evenness of being. My steps are no longer disorderly and swaying every which way. They now have a greater meaning to me. They are purposeful. Knowingly so. And where am I going? I am going to fulfill my destiny where the order of the day is joy and freedom. I am going to do my God's bidding, which is precisely that. To create in joy and freedom.

It took me half a century, doctor, to figure this out. And now that I have, my life is mine. No one can have any influence over it any longer, save my consciousness.

Yes, doctor, we have to go beyond this night.

Hopefully, the next time I meet you, it would no longer be in your office talking about pain and suffering, but on a playground, somewhere, conversing about kings and cosmos, and wondrous flights in the open spaces of imagination, the seat and source of all realized dreams.

IMAGINATION—the mother of science, the power house of all dreams, the muse of all inventions.

Next time, doctor, you tell someone: "You have a vivid imagination," realize that you are paying him/her a great compliment and, charitably, make that individual realize that as well, instead of considering it a shortcoming.

Yes, my dear doctor, it is high time to restore, and reinstate, everything in its rightful place. It is high time to recognize, salute, and respect what has sustained us for eons with such a formidable patience and forbearance despite of our abuses throughout the ages, namely MOTHER EARTH, WOMEN, IMAGINATION, HUMAN NATURE.

These are the power houses to be used, not abused, as a source of inspiration from which to create joyfully, freely, naturally.

NATURALLY, doctor. It is high time to salute nature. Yours and mine. In simplicity.

It is high time to extricate oneself from the entangled and complex web we know as social structure.

Why, you might ask, am I telling you all of this? Why are my grievances addressed to you, specifically? Because, doctor, you represent half of humanity. The male gender, at odds with the other half, the female gender. So that you may reconcile with and integrate within you the other half, the feminine aspect of yourself.

Also, and particularly, because you are a medical doctor. You are supposed to heal others. That is where humanity is at right now. An urgent need to heal itself and become whole. To no longer be separated, divided, ruled and controlled.

I am talking to you because it is my hope that you reflect truthfully on your personal skills and achievements as a healer.

I am talking to you as your ex-patient. As such, I am trying to heal myself and make peace with you.

Healing and forgiving, doctor, are key words if we both are to reverse this formidable downhill tumble that humanity has been engaged in for so long. If we are to reverse the cancer that is spreading throughout the body of humanity.

That is why I am talking to you. Or rather appealing to you, doctor. One soul to another wanting to integrate and embrace. One soul weary of conflicts and strife. Weary of prejudices and racism—there is only one race on this planet and that's the human race—weary of sexism and very bored, indeed, with all the "ISMs" conceivable.

"The issue in our world today is no longer about fission, but fusion," I read somewhere. Indeed, the crucial issue today is no longer separation, but INTEGRATION.

The anger I am voicing here, doctor, is because I care. Deeply. I care about uprooting, in whatever way I can, however small my contribution may be, the indifference and thoughtlessness that I see everywhere. Uprooting the collective feeling of powerlessness, fragmentation and loneliness. To become again a cohesive whole as a civilization; as an evolving species. To get out, at long last, after eons of programming, of this stagnating quagmire.

My nature, right now, my personal inclination, doctor, is to close this retrospection and resolutely march towards a hopeful prospect. That you too care as much as I do. And with my hand, fraternally holding yours, there isn't a thing in the world you and I can't achieve.

My personal prayer would be that you open your eyes, doctor and see me, perhaps for the first time, and recognize me as your own mirror.

When you do, you will become whole again and so will I. That's the way it works. We have been separated far too long.

You have to evolve into a loftier posture for me to evolve as well. Without you, I am incomplete. Without me, you are incomplete.

Enough of this nightmare! Enough of this night!

The day you make peace with me, you will have balanced the male and female within you, and on that glorious day, I will no longer be your target, but your mirror. In full partnership, in full understanding.

You will have, for the first time, grasped the full, the real meaning of healing.

Yes, doctor, HEAL THYSELF!

Do not give up. Do not give in, any longer, to the programming. Rekindle, in you, the initial flame of charity and justice. The initial commitment you once made to heal "in purity and holiness."

You can turn back the tide, doctor, from "dis-ease" to recovery. From chaos, to harmony. All that is needed is a change of focus.

The focus to heal, individually and collectively. All that is needed is the will to live. I want to live, doctor, as I know you do too.

Look at me, doctor, I am your mirror.

Your self-righteous posture triggered great anger in me. My anger, I fully understand, is not any better than your self-righteousness. We have to go beyond our respective attitudes, doctor. We have to salute and recognize one another. We have to be willing to change. For, I realize now, we are both victims and tyrants at the same time. And we need not be either.

There is this passion in me, doctor, that says: some day soon, we will all break through the tight grip of social conditioning into the open spaces of freedom. To breathe again. To inhale and fill our consciousness with the revitalized thoughts of health and reconciliation. To go beyond this night and wake up to a new reality.

To start a new page in the book of evolution. A new page in which we articulate the understanding of our accumulated and collective wisdom. A new page where we recognize and acknowledge one another as equals and individually unique.

A new page where we salute one another with admiration, for we survived it all, and because we did, we are all empowered, we are all worthy of respect.

A new page that says, unequivocally, how very powerful each of us is. And that, indeed, is a humbling thought, for it brings a new understanding.

The understanding that power and humility are two words signifying the same thing. One within the other. Power has nothing to do with having dominion over anything, or anyone. The real meaning of power is humility.

In humility, we recognize that each of us is a cell in the body of humanity. As a cell, we each perform a specific and vital function that contributes to the health and vitality of the whole body. A unique function that contributes to the development and evolution of the body of human kind.

Heal thyself, doctor, that's the only way you will be able to heal anyone else.

Yes, my dear doctor, this passion of mine tells me that this nightmare is about to end.

In anticipation of that day, I salute you, doctor, compassionately, lovingly, fraternally.

See you at dawn!

* * * * *

Several months after I wrote "A Word of Advice to My Gynecologist," I read a book that compelled me to write a postscript to my gynecologist.

Postscript: A colleague of yours, Dr. Robert S. Mendelsohn, declares in his book, *Mal(e) Practice, How Doctors Manipulate Women,* that a surgeon has been trained to operate. Therefore, he will uncover any possible loophole that will allow him to practice his trade: to operate. Even if it is not at all necessary.

"In my years of practice," says Dr. Mendelsohn, "I've seen a lot of surgery performed because surgeons believe that God blundered mightily when He created the human physique. You are supposed to regard it as providential that they are around to repair God's mistakes."

What do you think of those allegations, doctor? Have you read his book? No? Allow me, then, to quote what he says about surgeons in general, and male gynecologists in particular:

"Modern medicine still views women as doctors always have: 'as weak, nervous, hysterical creatures, subject to all sorts of psychological ills related to the female anatomy.'

". . . some profound historic reasons have made sex discrimination more virulent in medicine than in any other field. As far back as Hippocrates' day, . . . doctors believed that the female reproductive system was a source of hysteria and even insanity. For more than two thousand years, if a woman stepped out of the expected pattern of subservience and humility, her ovaries and uterus were blamed.

" The term HYSTERECTOMY, in fact, derives from the Greek word for hysteria (hysterikos) which means SUFFERING IN UTERUS. Thus, to remove the uterus was to relieve the pattern of hysteria."

Fascinating information! Hysteria today, doctor, as far as I personally know, is not treated by a gynecologist, but by a psychiatrist! Oh boy! Are we in trouble!

In another section, Dr. Mendelsohn talks about Dr. Sims, a general practitioner in the South in 1835. This is what he says about him:

"Anyone who closely observes the reckless intervention that prevails in obstetrical-gynecological practice will conclude that Sims is an appropriate choice for recognition as "the father of gynecology." His obsession with surgery and his lack of compassion for women who endured the incredible torture he inflicted on them are still reflected in the behavior of many who practice this specialty today."

I could easily quote the entire book to you, doctor, for the magnitude of the allegations and information in it are, indeed, mind boggling. It certainly shows me how blind I have been, as a woman, all my life. It is indeed a miracle that intuitively I felt compelled to recover from my blindness. That intuitively I have always felt suspicious of the medical field.

Every woman who has any measure of self-worth should read Dr. Mendelsohn's book. It is overwhelming in many respects, but nowhere near as overwhelming as our ignorance and oblivion, as women. It is about time to take a closer look at those who are in charge of our health.

Yes, doctor, these are very painful facts. But it is not too late to remedy this state of affairs. All we have to do is reflect genuinely on our motives and who we really are.

FREEDOM

I no longer want to work for a living. I want to live for a living.

I was given life as a gift from God, freely. So why should I attach a price tag on what God has given me free of charge?

I was given life, because I deserved to live. I earned the right to live. So, why do I have to earn a living, since I already earned it by being born?

Earning a living, what a ridiculous concept. I wasn't born for that. I was born to learn, explore and evolve. To experience in joy whatever I fancied.

Earning a living, what for? It doesn't make any sense to spend my whole life holding a job, so that I could pay my bills, so that I could remain alive.

Who invented that idiotic system? Who created these moronic social laws?

Well, I don't buy that anymore. I don't want to work so that I can remain alive. I want to work in what I enjoy, so that I can expand my mind and my consciousness into lofty concepts and undertakings. If I am preoccupied with paying my bills, there is no way I can achieve that.

So, what do I mean by "living for a living"? Simply this: do what brings me joy. Do what makes me happy. And what makes me happy is to play with words. Words are just envelopes for ideas. Blending them, chasing them, rearranging them—that is, to me, crackling my own bonfire. That's definitely my cup of tea!

What is the flavor of yours? If you find out and drink from yours, and if everyone did the same, can you imagine what a flavorful and joyful world we would have!

I drink to that! To joy!

I also want to travel on this beautiful planet anytime, anywhere

I please. All these borders and barriers, all these walls stopping me everywhere!

This planet is my home. It is humanity's home. This planet is our mother, so all of us should be able to go in our mother's house from room to room—country to country—and not just be confined to our room, or border. We are all brothers and sisters. We are all part of the same genealogical tree: humanity. Our diversity, our respective modes of self-expression, is our true beauty. It should not prevent us from meeting one another freely, everywhere.

I can't imagine telling one of my brothers or sisters to stay in their room at home; in order to venture outside of it and throughout the house, they should ask for permission. Why are there borders, anyway?

Perhaps, somewhere, in the dawn of history, a poor misguided soul arrived at a spot, put a picked fence line around him and declared: "This is mine." Having declared that, he put someone in front of his gate to protect his claim. The next thing we know, other misguided souls did the same thing and very soon everyone posted guards in front of their acclaimed territory. Subsequent quarrels ensued over what belonged to whom and somewhere down the line, one sad morning, we realized that this poor planet had been sliced like a pumpkin, with its seeds constantly scattered and rescattered, blowing every which way the warrior of the day will breathe.

You know who I'm talking about. Those yahoos called Attila the Hun, Genghis Khan, Napoleon, Hitler. To name just a few. Poor souls, there must have been a deficiency in the chemical composition of their brain. Anyway, thanks to them, boundaries were delineated, walls erected, fortresses built, and armies born out of the territorial attitude of the first misguided soul. And all this agitation was subsequently given a fancy name: History. His story. And what a story that has been! Talk about blindness!

And here we are. Submitting and obeying this crazy and unnatural state of affairs, otherwise known as "national borders," so deeply ingrained in our collective psyche, that we automatically and mindlessly submit to it.

National borders, nationality. To be proud of belonging to this country, or that one. To be nationalistic. What a baboon concept! What bafoonish pride!

Snap out of it!

It's like an individual's home. To love, embellish, develop and beautify my home is a great joy to me. But I wouldn't die for it. I just want to live in it, because it's convenient; because it's fun in that moment.

Besides, I don't have enemies. Enemies are born out of closed doors, closed territories and especially closed minds.

When all doors are naturally and freely open, there is nothing to force open. Is there?

I want to be as free as the birds. For, I don't suppose that the birds who are flying to warmer climates apply for a visa prior to winter.

Why should I?

Most people would declare that I am crazy.

In relation to whom? Is my answer. What is the point of reference by which I should measure my sanity or lack thereof?

Does the opinion of the majority constitute sanity?

And how did that majority acquire their collective opinion?

They acquired it through programming! That's how!

Didn't George Bernard Shaw once say, "There are mad people everywhere, even in mad houses."

And mad houses are managed by sane doctors?

Well, I let you decide that one!

PANDORA'S BOX OR ALADDIN'S LAMP
A MATTER OF PERSONAL CHOICE

The greatest waste of energy in life is the feeling of guilt. That waste of energy could be put to a better use. Namely, the pursuit of self-knowledge. Indeed, to be willing to open one's Pandora's box. That mysterious, notorious, mystifying box, buried deep within one's heart and subconscious mind. If we were to examine its content and, thereby, discover and learn what's lurking inside, we might be able to overcome the inner conflicts that are raging within and tearing us apart. By having a look at what appears terrifying to us, we just might find out, after examination, that it was nothing more than overblown problems, neither worth such worries, nor such waste of energy.

The desperate efforts we make to keep the subconscious door tightly shut, year in, year out, weaken our arms and enthusiasm.

If, instead, we were to open that door, we would see the cobwebs in which all kinds of stagnant dogmas and programming have become entangled, together with our prejudices, dissatisfaction, jealousy, rage, intolerance, hatred, impatience, misgivings of every kind. In other words, all the snakes that are shaking up the box and stifling us in the process.

If we were to vent off all these feelings, if we were to expel all that unhealthy swarming, we would realize that the source of all these entangled knots was our fear, reinforced by our guilt.

Fear and guilt are twin sisters. We can easily confuse one for the other. They blend with one another and dance with the vipers and snakes that sneak and crawl within the human envelope.

And the endless chatter and whistling of those snakes, shooting their poison within us, anywhere they can, transforming that corrosive poison into deadly diseases: AIDS, cancer, ulcers, cardiac arrest, atony and atrophy of all kinds. It makes one lose one's voice and breath.

Those snakes, constantly whistling to our ears, making us deaf to the most basic common sense, oblivious to the obvious. Namely, that all physical disorder, all diseases have a psychosomatic origin. And so, when incapacitated with any of them, if, instead of running to the doctor, we stopped for a moment and looked within—if we were motivated enough to find out how it all came about and what triggered it—we would clearly see the conflicting signals we give to our brain.

So, when we are confronted with a problem and our attitude regarding its solution is ambivalent, often refusing to face that problem, we push it, we bury it in the subconscious mind. We push it below our awareness and, in turn, our subconscious mind reacts violently against the intrusion of that poison and serves it back to us as a materialized problem: a serious disease.

That disease becomes, then, the temporary solution. It occurs to no one that people fall ill by choice. Subconsciously.

Anyone who falls ill has refused to face her problems and take responsibility for her life. She hides behind her illness—which frees her further from responsibility. She surrenders her power, instead, to the doctor, who takes charge of the situation. Having become ill, no one will dream of overwhelming her any further; her illness is her security blanket, so to speak. Because then, everyone pities her, consoles her, comforts her. And the irony in all of this pitying and petting is that we act against her own interest, making her more helpless.

And so, once she is healed from that disease, she triggers and falls prey to another, and on, and on. The greatest manipulators of all people —perhaps unknowingly—are those who are physically ill.

They seem to tell us: "You take care of me." "You nurse me and do everything necessary for my well-being."

In their silent manipulation, they play on our guilt to the fullest extent possible. Their poignant need for attention, their poignant need to be the center of our attention, is their own way of retaliating on those of us who have the gall to pursue our own happiness. Those of us who try to overcome and attempt to fly above the murk and the mire. Instead, they try to clip our wings, to ground us down to their predicament. And more often than not, we give in, give up our flight and crawl back, with them. Because we do not like to be labeled selfish.

Selfish. An interesting word. I am certainly selfish, now. It took me a very, very long time to become that way. I put myself on the back burner for a long time indeed. Everyone else, but me, was on the front burner. I took everyone's needs into consideration but mine.

But now I have changed. I have become selfish. Unashamedly so. Unapologetically so. I am Self-ish, for I am indeed in hot pursuit of Self. As the popular song goes: "It's my turn to see what I can see, this time is just for me." Yes, indeed.

So, coming back to diseases. All emotions, all thoughts, trigger a cellular mechanism that translates, depending on whether the thought or emotion is negative or positive, into a harmonious song of the molecules, or, on the contrary, a war between the cells within our poor body that is baffled to be treated so badly. Our body whose aim is to honor us with perfect physical health.

Everything is in the attitude and the command we give to our brain. That command is constantly made manifest in the body. Sluggish or lively, healthy or diseased, the body obeys the command. Absolutely.

Ah! If everyone made the effort to dive within, being motivated by a strong desire for her well-being, instead of constantly inflicting pain to herself, literally; if she made the effort to look at her inner wounds, she would be able to overcome her physical problems and finally discover her own physical and spiritual strength. Her own nature would reveal the magnitude of her own potential.

Making the effort to look within requires a great deal of willpower, to be sure. Indeed, it requires a lot of courage to look at one's fears and to overcome one's inhibitions. But when one does, the results are spectacular. Having expelled from one's system all the poison that was weighing on it so heavily, one suddenly feels much lighter and freer. One suddenly experiences an abundance of energy waiting to be fully used and demonstrating one's power, beauty and great potential.

With the tremendous release that results from this inner cleansing, comes one's awareness—the echoes from the huge reservoir of one's spiritual knowledge that would not have been experienced otherwise.

Having made peace with herself, she feels a great joy arising in her. Then, the obvious will occur to her. She alone has the power to transform her Pandora's box into an Aladdin's lamp. The miracle of this great alchemy comes about through the exercise of willpower.

And so, depending on her individuality, nature and inclinations, she can create a world uniquely hers. A world that matches her wildest dreams, for her benefit and the benefit of those around her.

Any individual who attempts to expand her mind, to heal, and come to terms with herself, automatically enriches her fellowman.

Ah! if everyone agreed to make that effort, that commitment to Self! There would never be diseases and therefore no need for doctors. Doctors would have to find another profession. Instead of perpetually maintaining this mass propaganda called preventive medicine.

Taking responsibility for oneself, instead of empowering someone else with one's weakness.

The idealist that I am whispers to me that, one day, no one will have power over anyone else.

One day, we will all empower each other. How? By simply being who we are individually, uniquely, beautifully. Inspiring one another, empowering one another by our respective pursuits. By our mutual exchange.

Fear and guilt will have vanished completely, and we will discover each other for the first time.

In the diversity of our being, we will look at one another as equal and unique. We will look at one another, and see an aspect of the multifaceted Self.

You and I. Two cells in the body of humanity.

Everybody and I. Billions of cells in a beautiful body.

HUMANITY.

Humanity, beaming with radiant health and vitality.

INTUITION VERSUS REASON
AN ASSERTION OF FAITH

I do not need to go back to a University
    to listen to a Lecturer brainwashing me.
The most outstanding Professor I know is my Intuition
    that automatically and authoritatively leads me to the books
    that will give me the explanations, or the answers
    I happen to need at any given time in my life.

My Intuition-Professor regularly tells me,
    in no uncertain terms, what I need to know
    and what direction to follow in every situation.

Unfortunately, more often than not,
    I do not act upon the wisdom and sound knowledge
    of that Inner Voice.
    Simply because my Outer Voice and my Inner Voice
    somehow play cat and mouse with each other.

Centuries of brainwashing, in the doctrine of "Logic,"
    did that to my poor soul.

And that is a pity, a great pity, indeed.
Because my Outer Voice—like the University Lecturer—
Reasons, reasons, reasons until it is blue in the face
    with LOGIC,
    that famous bastion of the blind, deaf, and dumb,
    and all it succeeds in doing is pushing speculation and deduction,
Ultimately leading nowhere, as far as the individual
    and the collective needs are concerned.

Reason is an invention of men.

Men's ignorance.

We reason because we don't know.

We use our head and not our heart.

Our head intellectualizes, our head theorizes.

But our heart knows. It knows from experience.

It knows from knowingness.

A strong feeling in the heart says so. Unmistakably.

Reasoning is rambling.

Reasoning is putting a leash on one's creative impulses.

Creative impulses are spontaneous.

Impulses that spring and splash, naturally.

And naturally, they flow like a river.

Reasoning is calculating, speculating, evaluating.

   Slicing and fragmenting.

Intuition versus Reason.

One is no match for the other.

Both are in a different league altogether.

For one is shouting,

The other whispering.

Shouting is a sign of powerlessness.

Whispering is quiet assurance. Tranquil certainty.

Intuition versus Reason.

Peace versus noise.

Intuition, the only Professor that ever made any sense to me up to
   now, does not speculate, procrastinate,
      or even evaluate.

It DIRECTS, it SHOWS clearly.
Sometimes it even FLASH-LIGHTS what to do.
Because it knows, at any given moment,
   what one needs, where one stands, and
   where one has to go.
It never fails in its statement and utterances,
   because, unlike the University Lecturer,
   that I shall call the Outer Voice,
   it does not pound its fists on the table,
   or raise them in the air,
   as though chasing a hypothetical opponent,
   to drive a point across at all costs,
   or try to make one "see the light."

On the contrary, the Inner Voice,
   manifests itself in a subtle, gentle manner.
First, it makes its presence felt, softly, suggestively.
Then, once its presence is acknowledged,
   it defines certain contours and then, and only then,
   when it senses that one is serious about
   getting an answer to a question,
   it deepens its focus, permeates with light all its aspects, and
   beams a sharp image of the answer.

That answer becomes a vision,
   what is commonly known as a gut feeling.

This gut feeling, then, gives a truer vision
   than the most advanced bi-focal any optician can provide.
Opticians, and Lecturers. There is no difference.
They busy themselves only with outer vision and

the mumbo-jumbo of reason.
Opticians and Lecturers are both
   the Neanderthal of the human Spirit.

They only affirm what their temporal eyes can see and reduce
   everything to object-ivity.

Pascal, a great French Philosopher, once said,
"Le coeur a ses raisons que la raison ne connait pas."*

It makes one think about the wisdom of children,
like the "Little Prince" by another French writer, St. Exupery,
   who said:
"On ne voit bien qu'avec le coeur."
"L'essentiel est invisible pour les yeux."

*"The heart has reasons, that the reason doesn't understand."
**   "One sees well only with one's heart."
   "What is important is invisible to the eyes."

CHAPTER TWO

The Jolt: Facing Myself

THE JOURNEY

What I am studying right now is some kind of archeology. The archeology of the Soul. The exploration of my Self. The long and meandering journey that will allow me, one day, to arrive and enter, at long last, the mysterious territory of my Spirit. Digging and exploring that mysterious and bottomless well of information, called Self.

Going deep within and experiencing, layer, by layer, in the depth, in the descent of this awesome universe within, a universe filled with echoes, visions and dreams; filled with feelings.

At every stage, at every floor, in the depth of my being, I am gradually learning to recognize the levels I have reached so far.

Oh, I am still close to the surface. But I am plugging away, developing my inner senses—indispensable tools to recognize and see in that kind of environment.

And sometimes, in my dreams—my dreams have become some kind of a radar, pointing me to the right direction—I meet strange people, telling me strange things in strange places.

Let me share one of them with you. Mind you, I don't fully understand all my dreams. Sometimes, it takes me years to understand their meaning.

I had this particular dream about five years ago, and I am not quite sure I fully understand it. Allow me to narrate it and interpret the symbolism as I understand it so far.

One night I dreamed that I met a vigorous and very tall man. He was about thirty years old.

—30? 3 times 10, the completion and coming into alignment of each part that constitutes Self?

—10: the body

—10: the Soul

—10: the Spirit

The completed journey of the Spirit, Soul and Body = 30.

—Body, the world of matter. Body, the beautiful planet earth.

—Body, the vehicle for experience of Spirit, and Soul?

So, I met this thirty-year-old man somewhere in the desert; a very barren environment.

—the illusion of physical life and its barrenness?

And he said to me:

—Come, let's get out of here.

So, I went with him, and in the next vision in the dream we were side by side inside a scaffold that was made out of wooden sticks— very much like those used to build a house—and we were descending, slowly, from very high in the sky, as though the scaffold in which we were standing were a great balloon.

And when we finally landed on the ground, I asked him:

—What is your name?

—My name, said he, is Sketches.

—Sketches?

—Indeed.

I said good-bye to him, and was about to depart when he added:

—Come and visit me sometime.

—I will, I replied.

And I left. In the next image, I was going from one shop to the next, looking at the windows. The windows of opportunity? The windows of choices and probable outcome?

Where does one buy the tools and the equipment necessary to explore one's Soul?

In retrospect, I think that that scaffold was urging me to complete its skeleton, to complete the sketch. To turn the sketch into a full-fledged design? To beef it up, to build the whole structure, with my imagination, my passion, my will and my emotions. Like bricks and mortar, like building blocks in a house, my inner dwelling, inside of which, one day, in full alignment with the male within me, having come full circle with Self—male and female— one day I will understand what this journey of mine is all about.

How out there, and here within, are probably two sides of the same coin.

MONOLOGING ABOUT THE LORD
GOD OF MY BEING

You are very much on my mind these days,
Sweet Lord God of my Being.
My heart is overflowing with love for you and
Though you still remain a total mystery to me,
    I sense, more and more, your gentle guidance,
    your subtle suggestions filtering through me and
    giving me a sense of direction,
    giving me the feeling, for the first time in my life,
    that I am really going somewhere.
To a place called Understanding.
The understanding that I am beginning to absorb,
    through the powerful emotions and
    overwhelming feeling of the magnitude
    of your love towards me.

My sweet God,
I don't even have words to begin to tell you
What I feel right now.

The only language I can use to express myself, at the moment,
    are these uncontrollable tears and
    the sudden realization that, indeed,
    you are talking to me.

And the extraordinary miracle is:
    I am listening.
I hear you, my beloved God
    and your thoughts are, indeed,
    sweet to my soul.

Oh, you have been so patient,
   loving and compassionately allowing
   my agitations and stirrings.

And now I want, with all my might
   to be worthy of your love.
Because, all of a sudden, I realize
   the stateliness of your Being,
   the magnitude of your Isness,
   and you know something, my beloved God?
The more I become aware of it, the more humble I feel.

It is humbling to know that I, Claude,
   am loved in such a profound way
   by as powerful a Being as you
I want so much to understand, feel and apply
   to my daily life the magic words:
   "unconditional love."
For, this is what you have given me for eons.

Funny, how associations of thoughts and ideas work!
This morning I didn't feel particularly happy,
   and so, in your usual subtle ways, yet very persuasively, you
   suggested that I read again
   the poem I wrote about Ramtha.

Ramtha. He is such a wonderful friend of yours!
He is a wonderful friend of mine too!
He is your "Spokesman" said he.

I suspect that, while I am in his audience,

you talk to each other over my head. Literally.
I can only imagine the resigned and helpless gestures
    you exchange with one another, and the feeling of complicity
    that two friends generally share,
    over my slumbering, stubborn ways.

So, I read again my poem to Ramtha and while reading it,
    I suddenly felt the urge to write to you.

You wanted me to talk to you, didn't you?
Well, here I am.
Trying to unravel the powerful emotions
    that you stir in me.

You want to explain to me, I know,
    what I am to understand right now,
    by having me allow that understanding to flow
    through my pen.
Black on white. My emotions will then be as clear as day.

About Ramtha, I have been ambivalent towards him
    for quite a while.
But that's because he was mirroring to me my inner
    ambivalence.

Remember how uneasy I felt the first time I read
    one of his books?
It was *Ramtha Intensive, Change, the Days to Come.*
It was in May of 1989.
Reflecting upon it now makes me smile.
At the time, I was reading the books of Seth.

Another extraordinary entity who channeled his books through
    Jane Roberts.
Anyway, reading *Ramtha's Intensive*,
    literally on the wings of Seth, made me feel uneasy.

Why? Because it triggered an obscure and ridiculous fear
    in me that I was being disloyal.

Why did I feel that way? I really shouldn't have,
    for Ramtha and Seth are two brothers delivering
    the same message: "Behold God."

Oh, the books of Seth!
I have read every single one of them!
How many are there? Maybe twenty:
—*The Seth Material*,
—*The Nature of Personal Reality*,
—*The Nature of the Psyche*,
—*The Unknown Reality*,
—*The Individual and the Nature of Mass Events*,
Etc, etc, etc.

Those books started to open my eyes and my consciousness.
They were an absolute revelation to me.
I read them ravenously, like a starved soul
    who could never have enough of that spiritual food to eat.
Like a starved soul, who suffered from malnutrition
    for so long and had barely survived on the garbage
    that I had been fed with from time immemorial.

Raw and coarse religious dogma of the past.

History, written by apologists, difficult to swallow,
     especially if I consider that half of humanity is
     conspicuously absent from it. Women.
And who gave birth to the other half so that he can write
     it in History. His-story? What about hers?
You tell me, my sweet God.
A simple oversight about the backbone of society!
No wonder it is crumbling down.

Anyway, where was I?
Oh, yes! Politics, tainted and self-serving, hard to digest.
Economics, attempting to justify the unjustifiable,
     virtually unchewable.

Yes, I was entering into a totally different realm.
I was beginning to perceive a new understanding.
And I certainly didn't want to leave it.
I felt more at home in that abstract world
     than in the heavy world of illusions I was living in.

It was a world of light and beauty.
Reality beyond the physical senses.
A delicate non-ending meal, subtle to the inner palate.
Gourmet through and through.

And so, as you remember, when I finished reading
     Seth's last book
—and after such a gourmet meal I couldn't very well
     go back to sauerkraut. Could I?
I went frantically searching for metaphysical material from one
     book store to the next.

And that's how I discovered Ramtha.

For the first time in my life, I sensed profoundly
    that the material contained in those books was real.
It made eminent sense to me, and it was not my intellect
    who told me so, it was my soul.

Seth's words first and Ramtha's teaching subsequently,
    resonated throughout my entire being and
    had the miraculous effect of wiping out of my
    consciousness, for good, that lingering and
    nagging feeling I always had: a constant yearning.
I didn't quite know what I was yearning for
    but something was definitely missing. YOU!

Yes, I know, my interchange with you
    was not always on an even keel.
It was rather like a one-way relationship.
I was always demanding, bargaining, requesting.
I was the eternal beggar.
And you gave, and gave, and gave, again, and again,
    endlessly, tirelessly, generously, abundantly,
    unquestionably, without end.

And I do thank you, my sweet God, for your bountiful patience,
    blessings and protection.

But now, I realize that our relationship must evolve,
    must become more meaningful, on a fairer basis.
It is my turn to give. It is my turn to give to you

and surrender.
To be still, and listen.
I do promise to listen to you to the best of my ability
    and to do your bidding.
For your bidding is also mine.
Your freedom from physical bondage is also my aim.
And I want that with all my might.

By the way, I want to congratulate you, my sweet God,
    for the company you keep.
Your friends, Seth and Ramtha, are truly awesome.
I have often wondered if, while I sleep at night,
    you "party" and frolic with them in different realities
    and giggle or indulge in uproarious laughter,
    slapping your spirits silly—I was going to say slapping your
    thighs—over the human condition and the unbelievable ways in
    which we conduct our affairs.
I imagine your laughter with that of your friends,
    manifesting itself as merry thunder, lightening and
    rainy tears of joy in our earthly skies.
Well, down here, in our heavy world, we are glad
    to provide entertainment for all of you
    beautiful light entities out there in the unseen world.

Your mighty tears of joy are a blessing
    that drenches our dry seriousness
    with your rambunctious good humor.

Pardon my digression, dear God, I was just curious about what
    you and your pals do for fun.

When you feel like inviting me, please beep me up!
 I'm always ready for a belly laugh.
Just make sure that I remember it.
   With a lucid dream, maybe?
Anyway, you know what I mean!

Now, back to Seth. His books were a blessing to me.
They lead me to Ramtha's teaching.
Seth and Ramtha. Two different personalities, indeed.
Yet, what comes out of one and the other
    is an extraordinary capacity for love and compassion.
Compassion of such a magnitude that it dissolves one's defenses
    into a strong wish to merge and be on a par with it.

And now, sweet Lord God of my Being,
I am ready to face you by facing myself.
I am ready to undertake the thorough cleaning
    necessary to become one with you.
As Ramtha puts it, I am ready to "make my vessel pure".

I want to recapture the joy and exuberance
    that have always been part of my being.
I want to recapture the essence of the innocent and
    spontaneous child whose laughter resonates,
    like singing crystal bells,
    in the vast inner spaces that you occupy and uphold
Within me. Always.

MY PURPOSEFUL TEACHER,
A DETERMINED WARRIOR

Ramtha, the Enlightened One,
Spoke to my sleeping self endlessly.
He spoke to me on one level, two levels, many levels,
In the tenacious hope that his purposeful thoughts
Would find their way in my understanding.

Like missiles, he launched his words
In an attempt to pierce and
    shake my being out of its secular lethargy.

Nothing was past him, as he kept trying numerous tactics,
Many different levels and countless other ways, I am sure,
Though I do not quite comprehend much of it yet.

He engaged my doubts, cajoled my hopes,
Screamed at my stupidity and blessed my willpower.
He scorned my pettiness and raised havoc with my guilt, and
    to top it all, he mercilessly amplified my fears.
All the while watching me, from his unique perspective, wrestle
    with his admonitions and my inner conflicts.
Often having me confuse one with the other.

I became, indeed, thoroughly disoriented.
Yet, he pressed, pushed and urged me to face
What he called my "monkey mind."
To face my personal demons.
To weed out my fears, doubt, guilt,
Lack of courage, insecurity. Lack of all kinds.

The list goes on and on.
He was telling me to work diligently on my garden.
For, said he, it was an unmentionable wild bush.

For me to presume to be invited to Ramtha's garden and
Recognize the different botanical species of his thoughts,
It was imperative to first weed out my own garden.

Overwhelmed by the task of rooting out so many parasites
        deeply entrenched in my consciousness,
I just sat there, discouraged by such a sight.
He might as well have asked me to swallow the Atlantic Ocean.
He was, indeed, asking me too much.

And all I wanted was to see Ramtha's garden.
But how could I, with a cluttered vision like mine?
How could I see harmony anywhere, when there was so much
        chaos within?

So signified Ramtha, in no uncertain terms and
Somewhat impatiently.

One moment calling me hypocrite and
The next whispering softly "beloved entity."
Each name-calling piercing my heart
With his extraordinary compassion.

Each name-calling, planted in my being like a seed,
Developing, growing, expanding,
Until I was forced to see myself truthfully.
Until I was forced to examine all these parasites and

Weed them out.
Until I was ready to work seriously.

After much talking, teaching, repeating,
Day in day out, event in event out, tape in tape out,
Suddenly, something in me started flickering.
First ripples, then waves of emotions went rolling up
My heart and my consciousness.

I would weep endlessly one week and
Start singing heartily, the next.
Tears and laughter blending together
In an endless cleansing process.

Resulting from such stirring and commotion and
Feeling miraculously lighter
Suddenly, my cells started dancing exuberantly.
 My molecules gossiped endlessly with one another:
"What is happening, a new dawn?"
Neurons and protons, molecules and particles
Began planning a trip throughout my inner being.
Their energy level rising to an ever increasing state
To spread joy further, up the stream of the blood vessels,
Down the meandering veins.

Everything in me was in a happy state of alert.
Everything in me was in an expectant state.
Everything in me triggered tears and joy.

And it finally dawned on me
What Ramtha had been doing all along.

He was taking me by the hand and leading me
To the doorsteps of the Lord God of my Being.
And what a beautiful and mysterious door it is!

Gently, but firmly, I have started knocking on it.
Meanwhile, patiently awaiting a response,
My imagination is running wild
Over what the other side might reveal and unfold.
My imagination cannot even fathom
What exists behind that door.
But I have a little inkling from the specks of light
Already escaping and filtering through the door.
Specks of light letting me presume
     that I have yet to experience "the miraculous,"
Letting me presume what is in store for me:
A fantastic reality.

Ramtha, the Enlightened One Indeed.
For, in the midst of these expectations
That he has led me to,
I am already experiencing "a fantastic reality."
The reality of JOY.

A WEAK WOMAN
WITH THE HEART OF A TIGER

A wonderful teacher of mine,
Getting very impatient with me,
One sad day, as I played, rather angrily,
Blind man's buff in a stuffy labyrinth,
Called me "spoiled brat."
Not only that, but also he threw on my lap:
"You are a weak woman with the heart of a tiger."

Well, talk about acknowledgement!
Whatever did he mean, anyway?

His comment, as I now recall,
Was followed by a long silence, before he concluded:
"Grow Up!"

That silence contained, indeed, information
That I knew I had to decipher.
Like an invisible dome covering my entire being.
That silence contained a lesson I was urged to learn,
Or else remain, metaphorically, trapped under the dome.

Now, "a weak woman with the heart of a tiger"
Sent me reeling for many a day.
If I ever bothered with dictionaries before,
It was right then and there.
Encyclopedia Britannica, Thesaurus,
Abridged, unabridged,
No version answered my question or gave a description of "The

heart of a tiger".

In the midst of my frantic search
For a proper explanation of who I am,
A weak woman? I guess so!
With the heart of a tiger? Really?
And what is that?

One morning, sitting at my desk, my pen in the air and
My nose probing the sky—what do you know?
The face of my beautiful teacher appeared in my inner vision.
Looking deeply through me, he said:
"You don't get it, do you?
"Why do you think the answer is in a dictionary?
"You have not been listening very well, have you?
"No book in the world can define you.
Only You can do that!"

That would be Ramtha's answer!
So, back to myself. The only source of knowledge. For me.

I, the tiger. The tiger and I. Hm!

O.K. Let's reason this.

Tiger, a strong and powerful animal.
But, if I am a weak woman,
How could I be strong at the same time?

Now, I'm confused!
So, what else is new?

Weak, confused and strong.
A bundle of contradictions to be sure!

What else? Tiger, a ferocious animal.
Ferocious, me? I don't accept that,
For I am a regular pussy cat!
But isn't the tiger also a cat?
Yes, I'm pussy footing like one.
Indeed, a master procrastinator.

Tiger. Power of overcoming.
Yeah, that's me!
Ferociously determined to survive.
Ferociously determined to live.

Now, deciphering the silence. What did I unravel?
In my understanding, it reads like this:
"Love is not always seen as the eternal embrace,
"It can also be seen as the eternal pushing away,
"To allow someone to grow up.
"Compassion is not always the warm embrace and
"The soft sounds and the sweet words.
"Compassion can be like this:
"Don't you ever come up to a block again and turn around.
"You go beyond that block. Make your own change.
"That is also compassion."

Yes, indeed, Ramtha, I hear you.
A warm embrace, perhaps, is not what a tiger like me needs.
So, what is a tiger, after all?

A tiger has vigor. He is robust, yet agile.
Mentally swift and resourceful.
He doesn't know what binary means.
My woman's weakness does!
But my heart, my tiger's heart,
Is perhaps analogically sound!

A tiger is also aggressive and combative.
Ingredients necessary to survive and live.

So, my tiger's heart is endowed
With a powerful zest for life and
A hearty dose of vigor and stamina.
And what is my woman's weakness?
It is my cage. The cage of confined and limited thinking.
The cage of a programmed jail-bird.
Breaking loose from the cage of programming
Into the wide open spaces
Of my imagination.

Tiger. Wild and free. Quite so!
That's my heart without a doubt.
So, now, let's blend these adjectives together
And see what flavor we come up with.
A base of vitality, sprinkled with confusion and
A hearty dose of vigor and strength.
A dash of aggressiveness for good measure, and
The whole mixture slowly simmering in my life's cauldron.
And in time, going up in steam, weakness and confusion,
Gradually escaping and disappearing,
Living in the pot, a hearty and comforting meal to live by.

That's me. Indeed!

Like a tiger,
Swiftly and gracefully,
Running through experiences and goals,
Jumping over blocks and
Developing mental muscles,
I meander through life's twists and turns,
Steadily, steadfastly, swiftly.
Like a strong woman, with the heart of a tiger.
Indeed.

WHO IS RAMTHA?

For a long time I have asked myself that question. And while I followed his teaching with my heart and soul, I kept wondering about this enigmatic teacher who had become, for the past five years, a very important part of my life.

I cannot explain his existence with reasoning and logic. I can only try to convey the powerful emotions he stirs in me, and how his teaching—everything he says—resonates deep in my soul. How it has profoundly changed my life and outlook for the better.

So, who is Ramtha?

Ramtha is a powerful and dynamic Consciousness. An electrifying presence that galvanizes the soul and makes the spirit soar to ever increasing heights.

Ramtha is an entity, channeled by a beautiful and extraordinary lady, J.Z. Knight who, over the past eighteen years or so, allowed Ramtha to use her body to deliver, to whomever was ready to listen and willing to learn, a powerful message: "Behold God."

He calls himself "Ramtha, the Enlightened One," and also "Lord of the Wind." Indeed, he is the messenger of the "Winds of Change." For, in one single gust of teaching, he can blow away one's taboos, prejudices and entrenched beliefs, and reduce to smithereens all the dogmas and misconceptions one has been programmed to believe from birth.

His lectures pertaining to the laws of nature and to the laws that govern the universe are so far reaching, yet so self-evident, so profoundly simple, it boggles the mind.

It clearly showed me that my way of living and thinking was against nature and against my nature. His statements are very provocative and challenging, to say the least. Provocative in the sense that they induce one to stretch one's mind about the concept he happens to be talking about at any given lecture. Mostly the concept of God—not God out there, but God within. The wondrous and enigmatic Self. One's Spirit.

But to me, the most powerful and fascinating aspect of what he teaches is also what he is not saying. Long after a lecture, there is this lingering feeling about unfinished statements, or sentences that remain floating somewhere in the mind, as though a pool of probable answers has been created by him, for us to retrieve, if we make the effort to do so. Like at a concert, the silence that succeeds the end of a beautiful symphony, immersing the heart and soul in a feeling of wonder and beauty.

And so, driving back home after a lecture or an event with him, one is wrapped up in a feeling—an atmosphere that feels like a thousand floating, silky, ribbons that are suggestive to the mind, teasing the imagination, tantalizing the spirit, like a thousand questions. Sometimes, it took me over a year to decipher the content of that silence and another year, at least, to figure out what he said.

Why does it take so long? Because his teaching is not a philosophy. His teaching is living the word. Experiencing the word. Then, and only then, could I understand what he is talking about. Otherwise, it remains a theory, a philosophy, a mere intellectual speculation that doesn't have any meaning unless I have experienced it, internalized it, felt it, absorbed it and turned it into an inner substance that becomes my experience and my understanding. Truth, wisdom, as Ramtha keeps saying, are not about words. They are about feeling, and living the word.

Yes, Ramtha, I am in kindergarten learning how to read in your consciousness, in order to understand what is written in mine, and spell it out to myself.

Boy, do I have a long way to go! From kindergarten to university. From the density of matter to the reality of the ethers. What a distance! A worm contemplating the flight to the heavens.

Yet, I know today, thanks to Ramtha, that such a flight is quite possible. The worm, in time, can evolve into an eagle.

In the meantime, I have to raise my head and start by climbing the tree. The tree of human life.

How in the world could I possibly understand what's out there, if I haven't the foggiest what's within me? What "within" is made of?

So, back to my reality. To my worm status.

The core of Ramtha's teaching is "consciousness and energy create the nature of reality." Which means that we are endowed with the power of making our life whatever we wish it to be. We are not, and never have been, victims of circumstances. If we think we have been, it is because we allowed it to be. So, it is up to us to reclaim our power over our own fate and put it where it rightfully belongs. Within Self.

It took me nearly three years to accept that concept and make it my truth. It was much more comfortable for me to believe that I had not much say in the events of my life; that I was manipulated by all kinds of external forces; that it was easier to accuse and lay the blame on others regarding my personal life.

Ramtha disturbed and ruffled up that belief of mine, thoroughly. His boldness knew no boundaries. His deftness as a tactician was sharper than a surgeon's scalpel, cutting through my excuses, procrastination, and what he called my monkey mind. Never mincing his words, masterfully adept in the art of unveiling and peeling off my objections and serving them back to me as lame excuses. From tears to laughter, from indignation to jubilation, from anger to peacefulness and all the nuances in between, he triggered in me the whole gamut of emotional upheaval possible. For there was not one single button in me that he overlooked. He pushed them all, firmly, deliberately.

Talk about being thorough! And as he kept saying, he never missed anything. Boy, do I know that!

So, when I got angry at him for relentlessly telling me that I am responsible for my life, when I didn't want to hear anymore of this, when I chose to sleep instead and ignore that he even existed, I started to find faults with him.

Yes, he was my mirror alright, in every respect. He was everything I perceived myself to be. And in those moments, I could not find enough derogatory words to throw at him. I denied everything about him. I even denied the emotions that his teaching triggered in me. I was mad indeed. How could I be so intensely worked up by someone I could not even see with my eyes?

How could I not? He disturbed my comfort zones, the cozy status quo of my life, and he had no qualms about whether I loved or hated him. That was irrelevant. What mattered was to look at myself, look at my anger, look at my reactions. As a teacher, he set himself as a target, a sounding board, a measuring stick, a blatant reflection, a powerful mirror. Projecting "me." Only "me."

He allowed it all. He designed it all. He provoked it all to get me to feel, to react and look at my reactions. Understand them and go beyond them. To transcend them. And when I was not ready for all of this work, my reaction was to call him every name under the sun. Among other things, a scheming, conniving, son of you know what. The devil lurking in my consciousness. A snake poisoning me with what I refused to absorb. Making me throw up, literally, the poison of truth that triggered very strong reactions in me. Reactions of rage and anger, flaring up as impatience, restlessness, even hatred towards everything and everyone, engulfing me into pettiness and a judgmental attitude that he magnified a hundredfold. Yes, it was a poison alright. I had to expel it from my system.

And me who always thought of myself as a pacifist, he sure

served up all the anger that I stored inside, safely locked away from anyone's view. Not from his, that's quite clear!

His tactics were also a medicine that brought to the surface the ugliest and most disturbing rashes of the mind, the itchings and discomforts of the soul that made me thoroughly restless. Because it made me realize that all the garbage I was carrying inside was indeed a heavy load. But getting rid of it required too much effort on my part. To even begin, I had to mobilize all the willpower, strength and physical stamina that I could muster and I didn't think I had what it took. I didn't want to bother, I didn't want to look, I didn't want to see. I didn't want to listen anymore.

Why should I listen to him? Who was he to talk to me like that? And so, when I was in that frame of mind, I became more blind. Because I chose to find him unreal. Wallowing in my self-pity, anger and rage was more real. It was what I knew best. It was familiar territory.

Besides, he had plunged the sharp blade of truth into my being—the truth of my insignificance, of all my petty and meaningless considerations—it hurt too much. Ignorance and my garbage were a blanket that had kept me warm all along and now, with a deft blow, he had removed it. He was telling it like it is and I could no longer resort to ignorance as an excuse. He was, indeed, a formidable teacher.

Sometimes, there was also this poignant need in me to be acknowledged and recognized by him. My contradictions knew no bounds. It seemed to me that he talked to everyone else and ignored me completely. His aloofness and silence towards me were very baffling. Sometimes, I longed so badly to get a response from him, a personal response, only to be more ignored than ever. It was a dizzying silence, a deafening silence, a hollowness inside, a sinking feeling of worthlessness.

I was to learn a great deal from that as well. And the lesson was that I was not to make him my new crutch, leaning on him and relying on his help, but that I was to rely on myself and myself only. He was there to teach me how to help myself, in every circumstance, in every situation. I was my only source of salvation and no one else. He was my teacher only to make me realize that fact.

He had also said once, at a lecture, that the best help he could give me was to ignore me. Only now, four years later, do I understand this tactic. Forever being a mirror signifying to me: I will acknowledge you when you acknowledge yourself. For, really, the price was not getting acknowledged, or closer to Ramtha, though it is part of it in a greater and more meaningful sense, but the priceless price was getting closer to self. To me.

I. I. I. A deafening letter, an obsessive sound, a sickening mystery. I had to get into it. I had to dive into it. To tear apart the veils and silence the uproar.

So, after I let my recriminations about Ramtha and myself simmer for quite a while, I considered what he had said and looked at myself. Evenly, truthfully, thoroughly.

Oh, boy! What a precipice! What a frightening hole! I lost my balance more often than I care to remember. That was not a reassuring sight. That was not a pretty sight. But I looked at it, I looked at myself and managed to withstand the gaze long enough to do something about what I saw.

A radical, a bold change of attitude was called for and ensued slowly, painfully, gradually.

Through Ramtha's guidance, daily I applied the specific techniques of "breathing" and "focus" that he taught me—techniques that became indispensible tools for my personal transformation.

Those techniques required all the physical and mental stamina I could muster.

First, the "breathing" technique, which he calls "the breath of life," the C & E technique (Consciousness and Energy), demanded every ounce of willpower I could find. Inhaling and exhaling willfully, sometimes two to three hours at a stretch, led me to a point of physical exhaustion, at which point my monkey mind was laid to rest. Silencing for a while the inner chatter and allowing me to reach a spot of inner peace and tranquillity that brought with it a feeling of renewal and inner cleansing.

After each breathing exercise, I felt such a sense of freedom and lightness, such a sense of exhilaration, that I thought I could literally fly. And I was flying in a way, for in my joy I could embrace the whole world and saw no flaws in it. Only beauty. And so, I wanted to extend that state of being, those beautiful moments that, at the beginning, were few and far between.

The second technique I learned from Ramtha, known in our school as "focus," involves sitting still for hours with my eyes closed. Sometimes, I sat still for many consecutive days, in order to reach a point of surrender and to allow the real Self to emerge. Allow the inner feelings to surface in my awareness and learn to observe them non-judgmentally, as one would see a passerby going his way. The goal was to arrive at a point of complete detachment that leads, eventually, to transcend all desires and destinations. To return to one's point of origin and centeredness: the inner Self from which everything radiates.

But before I could reach that point, I had to spent a few years disciplining myself daily to sit still with my eyes closed and seemingly do nothing.

It was quite a revelation to realize that the most difficult thing I could ever do was precisely to sit still. For I had spent most of my life in perpetual motion, always on the go. "I had to do something," "to be somebody" — whatever that means! — to justify my existence in a tangible way.

So, sitting still for long periods of time to silence my chattering monkey mind, to dissolve my impulsions, was initially quite a challenge. At the beginning, and for many months, I was fidgety and restless. In those moments of quietness, I felt the urge to move, to get up, to run away, to do something: eat, drink, go to the bathroom, walk around, talk, go to sleep. Anything, anything at all but sit still. I didn't want to content with my self.

Well, after a few years of practicing "focus," I managed to overcome the desire to run away. In fact, I learned to tame myself gradually and became, as time went by, quieter, calmer, more centered and far more peaceful. Sometimes for fleeting moments during that "focus," I became acquainted with that powerful force within—the force that had laid dormant for so long and was slowly waking up.

Stillness and silence taught me the art of becoming more attentive and patient. It taught me to allow my unknown self to manifest itself gradually in a myriad of ways, each way a flavor and potential to be realized. In Ramtha's words, "To make known the unknown."

So, as I applied these techniques on a regular basis, I gradually became aware of my shortcomings, my attitudes and the wrong postures that had colored my outlook on life. A very subjective experience, to say the least. I started to weed out the cluttered thoughts in my mind.

I came to the realization that I had always seen the world from my selfish perspective, never from the point of view of someone else. As I contemplated my reactions towards others, towards all those who pushed my buttons, little by little, I started to embrace a broader view; I was willing to consider the point of view of the individuals who were the object of my reactions.

In the process, I developed a detachment towards my reactions and saw others in a more objective and compassionate manner. For the first time in my life, I endeavored to put myself in the other's shoes. Consequently, I developed a more impartial attitude.

Indeed, instead of rejecting others, I integrated them within me. Each was a facet of who I was and to deny that was to remain in a state of self-rejection. Whatever quality I saw in another individual—good or bad—that quality was latent in me, or else I wouldn't have been able to perceive it in the first place.

Yes, for the first time I humbled myself to that realization and stepped down from my high horse. I started to view everyone from an equal and common perspective. Each of us equally trying to live and respond to our respective challenges in the best way we know how. None of us holds a monopoly on wisdom. All we can do is strive towards it.

Gradually, through intent "focus," I started to view each individual I interacted with as a teacher. Whether they were in my life in a casual or intimate capacity, each had a lesson to teach me. A lesson I had to pay heed to. As Ramtha taught me, no one ever comes to my life haphazardly, everyone is there for a specific reason. It was up to me to pay attention to what anyone had to say to me, verbally or silently, and derive an understanding from that interchange.

Yes, I understand a little bit better now. For me to dream about and ponder loftier concepts, concepts about what the universe is all about and how I personally fit in the grand scheme of things, there is an order of priority. Once I began to clear my mind of all its garbage and clutter, real knowledge could be received and translated into a broader understanding. I had to empty my vessel of its heavy load. The extraordinary alchemy about it is that the more I emptied it, the wider its perimeter became. Sometimes, after a cleansing, I felt so large and so light, that for a fleeting moment I felt very powerful.

I had a taste, a forerunner, of what was to come. A centeredness, an evenness of being, profusely sprinkled with joy. An expanding fire within that kept me going from one day to the next with expectations, motivation and exuberance. It had brought back to life the child within me who questioned less and experienced more, who doubted less and accepted more. Therefore, receiving more.

In those blessed moments, I was in a complete state of receivership. A state in which a large window opened in front of me, showing me an amazing vista for the first time. A vista where everything—sounds, colors and forms—became magnified, as though I had just recovered from blindness, seeing everything in its authentic light and beauty. Seeing nature in its true majesty. Because truly, for the first time, I had developed a sense of appreciation. Not only that, but sudden flashes of illumination, sudden feelings of acute awareness and knowingness, would seize me, increasing my understanding and making me see things in a new light. In a meaningful way.

And because of those wonderful experiences, I no longer took anything for granted. I was rediscovering everything. Counting my blessings and being grateful for such occurrences.

Subsequently, from time to time, I would ask: "Ramtha, who are you?" Curiosity made me wonder. After all, he was not visible. Nothing concrete to hold on to. Did it really matter?

In retrospect, I think that even if he had been a roach, if a roach had that kind of wisdom, mind-boggling wisdom delivered with profound simplicity; if a roach had that kind of patience, compassion and love, I was definitely going to be attentive to what that roach had to say.

Some have even suggested that it was no longer Ramtha's consciousness being channeled, but J.Z. Knight speaking. I salute you, J.Z., with my heart and soul. For, in any case, only an extraordinary entity like you could possibly channel a formidable consciousness like Ramtha. Like attracts like. And if it is no longer Ramtha, but you, J.Z., well, I remain speechless and very much faithful to such a formidable teaching. The teaching I am following is that of an extraordinary being. The name is beside the point, Ramtha or J.Z. It has nothing to do with names. It has everything to do with substance. And what I hear at every lecture, what I learn at every event, is truly mind-lifting, mind-expanding, and mind-boggling. And that spells WISDOM to me.

Besides, each time I enter the driveway of the school, my enthusiasm and excitement keeps increasing from one event to the next, one year to the next. Each time I am there, I feel a sense of exhilaration, a wonderful sense of anticipation. Because I know I would be richer for it.

These are the feelings I go by. This is the understanding that keeps me going for more.

So, Ramtha or J.Z., the only difference is in the perception; Ramtha and each of us in the teaching, the only difference is in self-perception. How big or how small each of us feels, that is the distance between him and us, him and J.Z.

We are so wrapped up in the forms and appearances of things—which are just illusions, anyway—that we often lose sight of the essence of things, the core of everything that is. And the essence I am talking about is feeling, wisdom, joy, love, understanding, tolerance, acceptance, integration, compassion, mercy. In one word: LIFE.

If anyone can put any of those values concretely in my hand and describe to me their weight, shape, texture and color; if anyone can make me evaluate and measure those attributes with my sight, touch, taste, hearing and smell, then perhaps we could argue what Ramtha's consciousness is. But we can't. Because it is without measure, without limit, without definition. It cannot be delineated within any perimeters.

Ramtha's consciousness just is. It defies the physical senses. Ramtha is. Like life is. He is life. Like you and I. Inextricably, undeniably interconnected through consciousness in an all encompassing continuum, in a never-ending expression of life. To grasp it, to understand, one has to develop one's inner senses: intuition, perception, knowingness. The language of feelings and emotions. One has to tune in within. That is where reality lies. Reality is intangible. It is impalpable. It is formless and weightless. For reality lies in the essence of things, in the spirit of things. That's what explains the material world and not the other way around.

Heresy all of this? Well, have it your way!

Life. What is life? Can anyone put that word in my hand and describe it to me? No. It cannot be described. It can only be lived. Yet, no one denies that life exists.

What is life? What animates the walking individual? What makes the sap run in the tree? What makes the river flow, the wind blow, the bird fly? It is the unseen, it is the intangible, the impalpable. It is the Spirit.

In my understanding today, the world of shape and form, the world of object and objectivity, the palpable world, are the illusions. A delightful illusion, sometimes an annoying illusion, to be experienced into delusion. I have deluded myself for a very long time. I now feel that I have come full circle. Reality and illusion, reality and delusion are part and parcel of the same circle, one giving the measure of the other. They are the two ends that close the circle, the two ends of the game of life to be played, experienced and enjoyed.

To believe. To be, and live.

To be lived. Self playing hide and seek with self. Blocked one moment by a question and gleefully dissolving it with an answer in the next.

And so it is. And so Ramtha is. Question and answer. One within the other, rolled into one; undeniably, beautifully, understandably, simply.

In the never-ending game of life. For, basically, when I am pondering the enigma that is Ramtha, I am mainly attempting to find an answer to the enigma that is me. The enigma that I am to me.

When I fully understand who Ramtha is, would I fully understand who I am?

In the meantime, I play hide and seek with Ramtha, hide and seek with me. For the heck of it, for the fun of it, for the intense curiosity of it. For no other reason than to play and to enjoy. To learn and understand. To expand and evolve.

Pondering turns into marvelling; wondering into discovering.

Consciousness to consciousness, seeking one another, helping one another, discovering one another.

And in this beautiful process, through this awesome teaching, the more I evolve, the more I mirror the limitlessness of his teaching back to my wondrous teacher . He is creating with his thoughts an unfoldment of my awareness; an unfoldment of my own consciousness.

The more I strive to understand the magnitude of Ramtha's consciousness, the higher I raise the level of mine; the wider I stretch the dimensions of mine. He is a facet of me. I am a potential facet of him.

Until one day, I will see eye-to-eye with him; eye-to-eye on the true meaning of life. Eye-to-eye in understanding, appreciating and loving.

Coming full circle with my search.

Coming full circle with my Self.

Coming full circle with Ramtha.

Circle turned into rainbows. Ramtha and I face to face, joining colors and understanding.

Ramtha and I. Two rainbows into the full and colorful circle of life, illuminating rays of joy, exuberance, jubilance, reverence for life. Saluting life.

To life, Ramtha!

Ramtha, the Enlightened One.

Ramtha, the Enlightening One! Infusing my being with the lightening flashes of his knowledge, the lightening flashes of his knowingness.

Discharging his electricity and energy into my being. Boosting me into a greater willpower. Transforming me into a doer, into greater creative endeavors.

Who is Ramtha? He is my magic mirror, blinking back to me a myriad of sparkling possibilities to chose from.

Projecting and deciphering all the knowledge and writings in my inner walls.

A masterful guide, leading me on a grand tour of my inner museum—going from one chamber to the next—explaining and spelling out, as we go along, the treasures and artifacts enclosed within me.

SOCRATES' ADVICE:
KNOW THYSELF

One of the greatest pieces of advice given to mankind was by Socrates: "Know Thyself." And it just recently dawned on me what he meant.

But, for a very long time, I have wondered about its meaning. "Know Thyself." How could I be me and see me? How could I do that? If I am Claude, how could I see Claude? I can't, unless someone else reflects back to me who I am by reacting towards me one way or the other. And even that is not enough.

So, what does "Know Thyself" mean?

It doesn't mean know Claude. For Claude is simply a vehicle through which Self experiences and learns.

What Socrates meant was: know Self, know what is hiding behind the eyes. Know the God within. As Ramtha would say: "Behold God." Know that powerful and motivating force, that subtle voice, the fire within, that prompts one to act and do, to dream and be, to explore and experience.

The God within that coaxes and cajoles me into loftier and grander undertakings that are just right for me. The awesome and powerful Consciousness that encourages me by beaming certain revelations in which I experience, for fleeting moments, inspiration and bliss.

The loving God within me, inspiring me and magnetizing to my presence and reality, all kinds of individuals and experiences that teach me what I am supposed to learn at any given moment. Pushing my buttons, or inspiring me. Valid lessons, either way.

And the more inspired I am by a situation, the greater my motivation, the more powerful and expanded the fire within.

The greater the fire, the greater the vision; the greater the vision, the greater the love and the more expanded the consciousness.

Know Thyself, indeed. For Self is limitless, boundless, ever changing, ever growing, ever evolving, ever stumbling, ever picking one Self up. Up and down the meandering path of life.

To love oneself. Moment by moment; one step at a time, until one wakes up from one's slumber and realizes that every experience is a game, an illusion, and laughs heartily at long last. For all that agitation was simply to "Know Thyself." To discover oneself through action and reaction. To see the whole game for what it really is. A grand play in which we are the scriptwriter, the director and the actor. Self performing for Self. In the grand theater of life.

Why? Because Self is a very playful child. Performing and giggling, playing and pretending. Playing and hiding. Playing hide and seek. Whirling and laughing in a never-ending spiral of experience, exploration and discovery.

Know Thyself. Self here, there, and everywhere, all at once.

Self, whose echo and song resonates and creates the lively dance of life.

.

SOLILOQUY

In all my meanderings, where does my soul hide itself?

Where are you, sweet soul of mine? Tell me. Tell me your story. Share it with me. I long, I yearn so much to know all that you hold within. How do I find the key that opens your door? Beloved soul of mine, please tell me. Put me to the test, you will see I can be a very attentive listener. I can truly tune in and pay attention. But don't just hint at things, spell them out. I want to know all there is to know. I want to know the full story.

Tell me, mysterious soul, as I am writing, what are you thinking? What are you thinking at this moment? What flight are you contemplating? Is there anything I can do to be a full participant in it? Tell me. Reveal to me. Confide in me your worries concerning me. Maybe I can solve them with you. What is not settled yet? I want to know. Help me, help you. Please don't let me ramble on indefinitely.

All I ask is to hear and learn. I have dreamt of you so many times, so many times I have attempted to understand what you expect of me. And at times I thought I guessed right, because it felt right. But at other times, I wasn't sure.

It was not an easy exercise, I will have you know. I wasn't sure if I was coming or going. I couldn't differentiate between my spiritual reality and the illusions of my physical life. My five senses are not very reliable, as you know. Besides, their perception and knowledge are very limited and this often plunged me into a state of confusion. I need so much to become your friend, to cooperate with you, to do your boss' bidding. Your boss, my beloved God, the sweet Lord God of my Being, of your being. But we will talk about him later. For now, let's see what you and I can do in His name. In His nameless sake.

So, as I was saying, all I can do right now is guess about you. So far, all you have handed me is just crumbs and, if anything, those crumbs have just deepened my hunger. So, you gave me some drops, but drops do not quench the thirst of someone who has been lost for so long in a parched desert. What is needed is a huge, tall drink. What is needed is a full meal.

I am reading so many books right now just to guess what is written in you. You are my book of books. My sacred record. My own Akashic file. When would your content be revealed and unfolded to my awareness? When?

I want my memory back, big time! You hear me? I am tired of you playing games with me.

Don't you think I have evolved enough for you to deliver more? Don't you think I am worthy of more knowledge? I want to know. I have the right to know. It is my book. It is my story. So tell me. I'm waiting. I'm waiting patiently. It is one of the qualities I am learning to develop, because I guess—guessing again—you are testing me.

Did I just fail the test? Perhaps, with this little flare-up. But listen, put yourself in my shoes. What am I saying? Excuse me, I lost my marbles. I know, you are not about shoes. You are much higher than that.

But how long can that patience be stretched? Oh, I get it, until I lose sense and track of time. But that could take forever!

What's forever? Boy, am I confused! Aren't you going to help me a bit here?

Let's be serious! Serious? That's not it either. Rather, let's be lighthearted. How does light pour into my heart? By making it less heavy. Yes, I've seen this picture in a book on Egyptian mysteries, where one's heart is put on a scale with a feather. That's how lighthearted I must become. Well, I guess, I'm overweight. I have to dissolve quite a few kilos. And what's the right diet for it? I know, you already told me. Patience, together with steadfastness.

Oh, well, where is this rambling leading me to? Let's find out. So, patience it is. O.K.!

I wait for your revelations, your encouragements, your instructions. I am in an expectant state. In a state of alertness. Is that a contradiction in terms? You tell me!

I, for one, do not think so. I, meaning Claude. Not the I meaning you, my sweet soul. For, at this point, I am consciously unaware of all that you know. But, eventually, I will know it all. Then I will be the I that is you. Fully aligned into one. Because that's what I want. I want the knowledge that is stored within me to rise to the surface of my conscious awareness, like emanations and vapors of I AM. I want the knowledge contained within you to flow out of my pen. One revelation after the next. Or rather one memory after the other. What fun that would be! I can't wait!

I want you to narrate to me the epic journey of your meanderings through time, the epic journey of my thinking through time. After all, I created it all. So what's all this fuss about holding it back? It's my book, and I shouldn't have to kneel down like this and beg to read it!

I could just see myself reading and reading endlessly in your book, in my book, directly, without having to resort any longer to outside books in order to trigger scraps and crumbs of feelings and vague memories. I want it clear and precise. I want it as plain as day.

So, what do you say? Don't you think I have evolved enough for you to start to open The Book. My Book? How about a peeping look into the first chapter? No? The first page? No? The first paragraph, then!

Oh, I don't like this. I don't like this fish market bargaining one bit. It doesn't smell good. I guess you don't like it either.

I can just hear you say: "Humanoids! When would they ever understand?" When would I ever get it?

So, when do you think I will ever be worthy of knowledge?

I hear you! Patience is the key. But—there is always a but—in the meantime, do you think you can show me the blocks I have to remove from my way? I am not trying to bargain with you here. But don't you think I deserve at least that much?

Give me a sign!

It must be fascinating to observe things from your perch. All I can do is crawl my way through endless meanderings and cracks. I am tired of crawling. I want to climb. I want to climb the tree of life and meet you at the tip top branch of the tallest tree. And, having connected with your heart there, I too will see from a loftier perspective.

What do you think of all of this? I think I have become flexible enough for you to give me some feedback on this.

In the meantime, I will tell you what I think from my perspective. I want to be very genuine with you.

You see, I am appealing to you, seeking your counsel and knowledge, yet at the same time, I am afraid of you. I really, truly want to know on the one hand, and on the other, I don't want to hear it.

Quite a dilemma!

Please, don't laugh. It is no laughing matter to me to play hide and seek with you.

I know what you are going to say. I am a bundle of contradictions. Well, suppose you tell me why that is. It is unsettling to me too.

I am full of enthusiasm and eagerness to know, to learn, to understand. I put it forth, I project it, I focus on it, but when I feel it coming, I sabotage it. I hide myself between my blankets and cover my head.

I know, it doesn't add up. I'm still crawling. Unfortunately. Where does this fear come from? The unknown? What is lurking in the unknown? Lack of familiarity? But familiarity is boring. As Ramtha would say "it is yesterday's news." So, why the fear of the unknown?

You know something? I am still an infant who cannot make sense of much, and completely engulfed in her wide-eyed naiveness. But one day, I know, all that will change. I just know it. Then, the veil will be lifted and I will become Claude the fearless. Better yet, I will become I AM the nameless.

And when that happens, when I have expelled all fear from me, you and I will be fully aligned with one another. Like the delightful story told by Ramtha about a child and a little genie walking side by side as friends; expanding and growing together. And then—let me dream on here—with the Lord God of my Being, the three of us fully merged into one, well, there is no telling what we would create then. With my finite mind, it's kind of overstretching me to contemplate infinity at this point.

Anyhow, until then, I continue to picture you as a big splash of brilliant light ejected from God's Spirit to venture, explore and discover. And like the story of the prodigal son in the Bible, bring back to the Father/Mother principle experiences and knowledge. "Making known the unknown," says Ramtha.

There is nothing more exciting to me than to learn and know. To discover and understand.

Finally, it may be that everything is very simple and that I complicate matters by design, to give me the illusion that I am doing something. Or is it that I am just heavily programmed by complexity?

Maybe true knowledge requires no effort. Only knowingness to be retrieved at the tip of the thought. All I have to do is relax and wait. Relax and be in a state of receivership. To simply open my heart and my mind to allow the exploring thoughts and revelations to splash in my being and emerge as understanding.

Yes, wait and be.

I remain, always, open to you.

HOUSE CLEANING

Over the past few weeks I have had the disturbing and uneasy feeling of stagnating, slipping away: as if there was no movement in my life. What was happening and where was I?

The answer came like a soothing breeze.

So, did I lose my will? Strange question! How could I? She is part of me. She must have gone on vacation, then. But she went without any warning, leaving me hanging there, wandering aimlessly and pondering why.

My heart did not go with her though. He stayed right here with me; consoling me with joyful memories, but also unfolding, stirring and churning powerful feelings and emotions for me to contemplate, so that I may heal while my lady Will is on vacation. That's the way it works. I understand now. When the will is on vacation, the heart gets busier than ever. He keeps projecting and showing me the things I have to look at and tackle earnestly. For when the will's vacation is over, she will be rested, refreshed, and happy to be back to work full steam on creating and manifesting. Manifesting what? Whatever!

So, she left for a while to give me a chance to do some heart cleansing, so that I may lighten up. For her to create and achieve, she requires a light heart. It is the only way she can fly.

Yes, Lady Will, I understand. Fully.

There are so many rooms and chambers in my heart, that I truly had to roll up my sleeves and settle down to work. So, I went to the supermarket to buy all the things I needed for a thorough cleaning:

—A duster to dust off the cobwebs of regrets, procrastination, doubts, resentment, laziness;

—Ammonia - am-onia - to dissolve the stains of guilt and fear that weighed so heavily on my heart, that it is a miracle it didn't explode into oblivion;

—A vacuum cleaner to blow out the prejudices, beliefs, piousness, self-righteousness, rigidity, status quo and programming of all kinds. Social, religious, political, medical, family pressure and peer pressure, all pressures. You name it. I'm vacuuming it!

—A pair of scissors to cut out self-pity, complaining, and accusing;

—A polish to shine and highlight, in their rightful place, the qualities in me that kept me alive and going. Qualities that I tended to forget in the midst of my chaotic and disorderly house, and

—Last, but not least, when all this cleaning is completed, an airfreshener with a fragrance made of a blend of joy, determination, and a new and light-hearted attitude that will entice my Lady Will to come back home happy, eager and willing. Willing indeed! That's her nature.

For then and only then, my heart becomes light, jubilant and squeaky clean. Ready to greet my lady Will back with joy and anticipation.

Then begins the duet singing and dancing of my Heart and Will in a never-ending movement of creation, in a never-ending expression of life.

CONVERSATION WITH MY IMAGE

One day, out of boredom, I got all dressed up. Ready to go. To go nowhere. But perhaps nowhere is somewhere. So I looked at myself in the mirror and this is the dialogue that ensued.

—Hi there! What's happening?

—Good question!

—What's the answer?

—Well, what do you want to do?

—Cheer up! That's what I want to do! 'Cause, frankly,
    I'm bored!

—I see!

—What are you doing?

—Putting on lipstick.

—What for?

—To cheer-up! What else!

—You don't need to put on make-up for that!

—Says who?

—Says me!

—You don't know anything!

—Now what? You are putting colors on your eyes too?

—Yeah! Make them bigger. Isn't it pretty?

—Another illusion. They look bigger, and blinder!

—Listen here. Don't you get pious on me. What makes you so
    sanctimonious anyhow?
    Everything is an illusion. We are here to play games.
    The game of life. So keep quiet and let me play!

—The cheeks too? That's too much rouge!

—Be quiet!

—Why did you put rouge on your nose?

—To look more natural!

—You are putting on a mask of make-up to look more natural?
  You've got to be kidding!
—And you think that without make-up I don't have a mask on?
  Boy, Have you got a lot to learn!
—Where did you get such a sharp tongue?
—When I had to answer to the likes of you!
—More rouge on your nose? What are you doing?
—Yeah, my pink nose gives the impression of freshness,
  as though I have been running in the woods all day long.
  No one will ever guess that I'm stuck in a box.
—What now, why are you bundling me up with this tight skirt
  and jacket?
—My, my, are we grumpy today!
—By the way, isn't that suit beautiful? Silk gabardine with a
  jacket pleated in the back. Sooooo elegant!
  You like this color taupe?
—Hm!
—You could pay me a compliment, you know, it won't hurt
  you!
—Well, I must say I like this silk blouse. It is very colorful.
  This blend of fuchsia, olive green, gold, black, and taupe is
  very becoming!
  The silk feels, oh, so very sensual!
—Well, I'm glad you are coming around and shaping up a bit!
—Are we going anywhere?
—Do we have to go anywhere?
—So why are we doing all this?
—Arguing again?
—Alright, alright!
—A broach on the jacket lapel? How shiny, how tacky! It is not
  even gold!

—So what?

—You don't make any sense! Silk fabric with fake jewelry!

—It's you who doesn't understand! I'm making full sense! I'm
   making full use of my physical senses. Look how fabulous
   this outfit looks. Feel the soft touch of silk. Feast your eyes
   on the bright colors. Smell the fragrance of the cologne on
   my clothes. It smells like the rose of the Sahara in North
   Africa. Exotic! Can't you appreciate anything?

—Hm!

—And if all of this is not making any sense, I don't know what
   is!

—You think you're pretty smart, don't you?

—Well, it's you who doesn't want to play with me. You're
   resisting everything I do! I'm doing this for a reason.
   I'm not sure what, right now, but I'll find out, somehow!

—High heels? Now, that does it!

—Relax, high heels make me look taller.

—Doesn't make you any smarter!

—That's your opinion!

—Now, we want to fluff up the hair and put that rebellious
   little lock on the forehead, just so!

—Ooooh, I look terrific!

—Ha, ha, ha, ha, ha!

—Why are you laughing?

—Ha, ha,ha, ha, ha! All dressed up, and nowhere to go!

—Ha, ha, ha, ha, ha! you make me laugh so much, tears are
   melting the make up away!

—See? That's why I dressed up!

—What do you mean?

—To make you laugh, that's what I mean! Remember how
   bored you were a moment ago?

My image paused for a moment to think.

—Indeed, I see your point now, she replied laughing, her face
jubilantly beaming, colorfully joyful, and open.

—You are right, there is no such thing as a frivolous activity.
After all, if it can bring a smile, laughter and joy, then,
indeed it has served a great purpose.

—I'm glad you finally agree with me, sweet image. You are also
an integral part of me.

—Friends?

—Friends!

IDLE CONVERSATION
WITH MY OUTRAGEOUS SELF

Well, now. Here I go again, in English.
It is nice to express one's thoughts in two languages:
French and English.
My French speaking self
Has adopted the English language.
But, English or French is just a superficial
    medium of expression.
The only language that is real is the language
    of feelings and emotions.
And words are inadequate to translate them.

To express in feelings, in thoughts,
That is a powerful language indeed.

In the next reality where I'm going—home—
Entities communicate with one another
In feelings and thoughts.
One entity thinks something and
    the other sees that right away.
Incredible. Unthinkable to apply that
    on earth right now.
It would be most destructive.

Right now I feel sleepy.
But this exercise - talking to myself -
    is a good discipline.
In what? Probably endurance.

I think, when I come back from my trip to Washington State and
    start writing earnestly,
      it will be more exciting, 'cause I will have to focus
      on a specific matter or chapter,
      and that way it will be more meaningful.

Who am I kidding?
Not you, my sweet God, I know that.

So, on with my idle thinking,
    floating like a leaf in the sea, and
    drifting, drifting, drifting endlessly.

What else do I feel this minute?
A sweet crystal ringing in my ears that says:
I'm alive!
Does that mean, it is also a sign
    urging me to wake up,
    or perhaps shape-up?

I wish I could.
But right now, I'm bored.
Yeah! I'm Bored out of my wits.
Nothing to think about. Nothing to say.
 Only this dozing, ruminating, feeling,
    coming and going nowhere.
A nebula.
An insipid and shapeless cloud,
Turning around and around.
Aimlessly.

Come on, snap out of it Claude!
Wake up!

My sweet God, I love you,
    but now, I'm having a dry spell,
    can you pull me out of it?

I am now looking at a picture of me.
Beautiful woman!
I love this woman.
Dry spell or no dry spell.
She is attractive, elegant, exotic,
    very immodest to be sure.
She has a beautiful smile
    that reflects kindness and perplexity
    at the same time.

Tell me, my sweet God,
    what do you plan to do about the perplexity?
Can't leave it there, can you?

Well, I'm not telling you what to do,
    but, hey, you know what I mean!

So this beautiful lady,
    dressed in royal blue silk,
    is the vehicle through which
    you are experiencing perplexity.
How do you feel about that?

Well, perhaps being perplex isn't so bad.

Time to take stock, think and reflect, perhaps.
That ought to clear any perplexity!
Right? To keep going again.

Coming back to this lady in blue—
    her husband and her children call her Queen.
Yes, there is something royal about her.
Probably her lineage and association with you,
    my sweet God.
But you see, royalty is not at all she is after.
What she is seeking, what excites her beyond words,
Is WISDOM. To become wise. To be wise.
That, to her, is an imperial crown.

Yeah! And what is wisdom?
Wisdom is feeling. It is knowingness.
    after one has absorbed the feeling.
It is that beautifully quiet place within
    that tells me everything is all right.
It is the joy and understanding
    that I am at the right place,
    at the right time.
That everything has its meaning
    and reason to be.
With time and patience,
    everything falls into place.

Ultimately, everything becomes self-explanatory
    and one kicks one's forehead and says:
But of course, that's what it means!

Even boredom contains wisdom.
To see the light,
    one has to understand the shadow.
For one gives the measure of the other.
One highlights the other.

Yes, beautiful, graceful Wisdom.
I love your nature greatly and wish
    to get better acquainted with you.
You're are my favorite Lady.
My ideal.
Come and visit me some time.

THE POWER OF SILENCE

My monkey mind is so used to constant chatter,
So busy gab-gabbing, that it is seriously impairing,
One of my senses.
HEARING.

Chatting and hearing are always at odds with each other.

Even in conversations and dialogues with others,
We never really dialogue with anyone,
We just keep monologing together.
Like a bunch of hyenas hearing nothing.
We just keep chatting and chattering,
Constantly clapping our teeth together,
Hardly hearing what the other is saying.
Always busy concocting a clever answer
To a question not even half-heard,
Giving less than half-answers,
And half-understanding.

And so, the collective music of humanity
Is an ear-splitting cacophony,
With tympanic piercing thoughts
Criss-crossing from one to the other.
Like missed projectiles,
Running off-target,
Bombarding one another,
Aimlessly and uselessly.

And this mechanical motion of the mouth,

Constantly ruminating rehashed thinking and
Regurgitating meaningless mumbling,
Leads us to a dialogue between
Dumb and deaf.

We all have, indeed,
A hearing impairment
That needs to be corrected.
Not at the office of
The Otolaryngologist—
What a word! That word alone
Would make me deaf and dumb at once.

No, to heal my impaired hearing,
I have to enter the clinic of silence.

Because if I don't hear,
I learn nothing.
So, I have started to shut my mouth and
Re-exercise the muscles of my ears.

Attuning them to the quality of Silence,
Gradually and softly, building up the decibels
To a comfortable level which I could hear.
Bells ringing into soft decibels and signifying
An adequate understanding.

The more I practice this silence,
The more I learn.
Sometimes, it is a real "Niagara Falls"
Of information that pours into my ears.

What others have to say
Is such a great lesson
To learn from and to hear.

And beyond that, even alone,
One hears a great deal more,
When one stops the inner chatter.
For then, the nuances of sounds
Around and within—
Well, they sound more subtle.
They are more informative.

Remaining quiet and silent,
One also hears distinctly
The language of feelings and emotions.

One hears Self.

Yes, silence is a powerful universe.
Abuzz with information,
With the subtle and unique music of Self.

The music of self,
A melodious concert,
Echoing the sound tapestry of self.
The power of observed silence
Rewards one with the music of the sphere within.
Powerfully, harmoniously, echoing Silence.

The sound of silence,

Sinuously sliding
Into a smooth understanding,
Feeling and hearing,
The power of Silence.

THE TRAPEZIST

I am an initiate in the school of life.

I am also a student in the "Ramtha School of Enlightenment."

Both schools are very demanding. Each one requires my full participation and understanding. One is in complete contradiction to the other. Yet, both are very important. They are both urging and teaching me to balance from one reality to the other.

The first one teaches me the hard knocks of the material and physical world, and though I get a lot of bumps and bruises in that particular school, I am taught that all of it is an illusion. Even when I am black and blue, the pains are nothing more than the importance I consciously give to them. No kidding!

The second one instructs me in the authentic reality of life, the essence and intangible aspect of that objective world, my consciousness. My consciousness is indeed the springboard, the launching pad as it were, of the first one. It is the "busy body" behind the scene. It is the creator of the scene. So, whatever scene I create will make me sink or soar.

To balance from one reality to the other, and to keep a sound footing in each, is no small gymnastics, I assure you. So, by necessity, I have become a trapezist. In the circus of life, it is very important to calculate every step. It is a do or die situation. I can't begin to tell you the contortions I go through in order to give the illusion of sanity and balance.

Mind you, its not all an illusion. Somewhere, along the way, I am learning and developing a certain balance. Being a trapezist is, indeed, a discipline requiring precision and economy of movements and thoughts. For, wastefulness of movement and thought leads inevitably to a loss of balance; sometimes a deadly one.

So, this discipline has taught me to become clear and precise on what I want before jumping. One gets far fewer bruises that way. One acquires greater mental elasticity in the arena of life.

My ambition is to integrate both schools fully and effortlessly within me.

To be able to swing gleefully and confidently, and fall on my own two feet in the grand and beautiful game of life.

WHO AM I? DEAR GOD, TELL ME

Here I go again, my beloved God, with my question.

Who am I?

I think it is high time to get an answer. An answer is long over-due. And may I be so bold as to request a promotion? Yes, I think I deserve one. To be promoted to the status of partnership with you, knowingly, in full understanding.

But, before I go on with my usual negotiating business with you, perhaps I need to recapitulate from the beginning.

This life of mine that you have created and set into motion, what a motion picture! I must admit, You have a great sense of humor. Reviewing this movie recently, I saw how incredibly unusual my life has been by any standard. Conventional standard, that is.

Boy, you had no qualms about whether or not you were overdo-ing it. You just drew the outlines and made sure I went through the motions. Talk about a spinning bee. Somebody once commented that I was like a whirling dervish. Maybe so.

Anyhow, let's review this movie as it unfolds so far. For, that is just the preliminary. I fully intend to go on for a very long time, with more awareness from this moment forward, and see what understanding I come up with. I trust you will clarify things for me along the way. Thank you.

Now, my entry into this world, my background family.

You landed me in Morocco, to Jewish parents, in an Arabic land, in the heart of the French quarter, where I grew up and attended French schools.

At my birth, five sisters and two brothers, together with my mother and father, greeted me, each in their own way. My eldest sis-ter was twenty-two years old when I was born. And so, I grew up in a family made of adults. They all loved me greatly, but somehow I felt stifled by so much attention. If one considers that I also had numerous uncles and aunts, who had each a lot of children, belonging to a tribe doesn't leave much room for individuality and self-expression. For indeed one has to conform to the collective behavior and patterns of thoughts of that tribe.

I understand what you were doing, my beloved God. You chained me in an environment, so that I could learn to break free from those chains. Mentally and physically.

So, each of my sisters and brothers had a different outlook on life; and each influenced me in a different manner. Some quite profoundly. But what was truly amazing was that each of them had a vastly different posture on life, as though each had come from a different galaxy. Bless their hearts all. I sure was swimming in a confusing emotional melting pot.

Yeah, I can still hear your great laughter, dear God, upon my landing: "You can do it," you said.

Could I? Not without a great deal of heartache and confusion.

I was brought up to be proud of being a Jew. Yet, I attended only French schools, where ninety-five percent of the students were French. I also lived in an area of the city where I was surrounded by French Catholics. The only place of worship in that area was St. Peter's Cathedral, whose bells resonated far and wide, reminding us Moroccans, Moslems and Jews alike, that only Christian faith mattered. Those bells muffled and silenced our beliefs and system of values.

Morocco, at my birth, was a French colony. Or rather, a French Protectorate. Protecting us from what? Our freedom, to be sure! The ruling class, then, was French. And so, when I grew up, being Jewish was not so hot, especially around World War II.

To French people, I was only a Moroccan, a colonized non-entity; to Moroccan Moslems, I was just a Jew. And so, fitting nowhere,

I withdrew to the only place I could. My imagination. There, at least, I had to answer to no one. On the contrary, they all had to answer to me!

But, don't get me wrong. I am very happy about the circumstances of my birth. You did a great job, my sweet God. You had me born on a Saturday morning—the Jewish Sabbath, a great celebration in my family—at 7:00 o'clock in the morning—my favorite number.

Anyway, that particular Saturday was a beautiful spring day, late in March, in a private clinic made of black and white marble. You wanted me to understand the meaning of light and shadow, right? That's why it was black and white. Also marble is a stone that suggests polish to me. The polishing and refinement of experiences into wisdom?

The name of the French doctor and owner of that private clinic translates into English as "Wood-Rock." Interesting. Wood is a natural and soothing element, and rock is suggestive of firmness and solidity.

So, I was helped into this world by a doctor whose name meant natural firmness and strength. In retrospect, I can now see that I had a strong dose of willpower.

It was also interesting and quite significant that my Jewish parents began to celebrate Christmas when I was born. All the wonderful toys I found by the chimney! The one I remember most vividly was an electric train. I was fascinated by it for a long time. I now understand why. It was my subsequent train of thoughts that kept me electrified and alive. Even though it was running around and around on the same track. That's why you had me derail periodically by the crises you sent my way.

So, in my early years, I registered and internalized very conflicting instructions. And my desire to please everyone and be approved by all of them—truly an impossible task—created formidable conflicts in which I tried to be everything to everyone. Later in life, I developed an attitude of defiance. For the many choices I made in my life were exactly the opposite of what was expected of me by society in general, and my parents in particular.

Not to mention the formidable crisis of identity I dragged with me all my life. Indeed, the most painful aspect of my life. I didn't fit anywhere. Because of the manipulative forces that put different ethnic groups at odds with each other, hostility and racism were rampant all around me.

But, this difficult state of affairs was tempered by the bountiful love and unconditional acceptance of both my mother and my father. It made swimming against the tide more bearable as I was growing up. My parents had an attitude of grandparents towards me. Very lenient and very patient with my sense of revolt.

But you, my beloved God, you forgot to tell me that all these circumstances were simply a stage in which to perform and play. To play a particular game. So, for a long time, I played very seriously. Dead serious. Was that a negligence on your part, or a sin by omission?

You don't believe in sins. That's right! Another dogma that got dumped in my life's script.

Anyway, I realize today that all of this was a blessing in disguise. For it developed in me a great deal of resilience and willpower. The will to distance myself from family programming as well as political programming, and to question them both as I grew older. The will to overcome whatever situation life threw on my lap, because I was, by nature, joyful and exuberant. I had, against all odds, an optimistic nature that nothing, ever, destroyed. But that was because of the abundant love I was greeted with from birth, which gave me a solid base in life. I felt important, because I mattered to nine individuals. I mattered a great deal, to this very day, in fact. And that, truly, is the greatest blessing of all. For, despite my revolts and reactions as I was growing up, my brothers and sisters always regarded me as a fanciful, original individual whose unexpected whims kept them guessing and wondering, yet they treated me with great fondness and affection. My eldest sister always called me "a ray of sunshine."

And yet, as I was growing up and observing each of them from a child's perspective, I recall thinking that their deeds didn't match their thoughts and instructions to me. Somewhere, deep in my soul, I felt very sad and sorry for them. Somewhere inside, I felt and understood their inner turmoil. And so, early in life, I made the decision that I was never going to become an adult. The world of adults didn't make any sense. It appeared very chaotic and confusing.

That's perhaps why, throughout life, I retained my child-like characteristics, my spontaneous nature and naiveness, and often bewilderment, in front of life's slapping waves that threw me out of balance more often than I care to remember.

In my childhood, my sisters were the authority. Whereas both my mother and my father were my friends, they made no demands on me. I remember many wonderful and quiet moments spent with my father, who was also an avid reader. He often commented to me, as we were both sitting by the fireplace, on the book he happened to be reading. He too found great refuge and solace in books. As for my mother, everything I did was cute and wonderful as far as she was concerned and she truly loved me unconditionally.

Yet, looking back now, dear God, I can see that from very early on in life, you made sure that I was never completely satisfied. You didn't want me to be complacent for too long. So that I would constantly try to renew myself by trying and experiencing new and different things. Boy, was I ever!

You had me zigzagging emotionally and geographically throughout the planet and across my inner being. Swinging wildly outside and wavering endlessly within.

You purposefully triggered periodical crises in my life. They manifested themselves like clockwork. It was as though I was keeping an appointment with Self, in order to take stock and reassess what I had been doing between appointments. Between you and I. The core of the crisis was always the same:

—Who am I?

—Where did I come from?

—Where am I going?

—Why am I here? For what purpose, and on whose decision?

—What is life all about?

Clearly, in each instance, I was completely lost in the game, in the illusion I was enacting. Otherwise, I would have had enough detachment to see it all. To see that life, in its essence, is pure joy. It is one laughter after the next. A divine comedy.

Life is indeed a hilarious joke, truly. It is an extended dream; a deep slumber.

And so, periodically, you woke me up with a crisis and made me look at that part of my game.

Lighten up! you said.

I did. I dried my tears and went on to the next act.

Anyhow, fickleness and diversity became part of me. One might say that my field of expertise is diversity. I subsequently became Claude of all trades. And I dare say, master of all.

I have been a translator. My translations were deemed to be better than the original and circulated throughout the French speaking world.

A Public Relations Consultant who could sell ice cubes to

Eskimos and make them believe they got a good deal.

A Conference Manager who coordinated the activities of all participants from one item of the agenda to the next, with the logistics of those activities thoroughly covered, leaving nothing to chance, so everyone was unaware of all the hard work invested in organizing it all. Like good health, one is unaware of one's body because it works automatically.

I have been a boutique manager and sold clothes like hot cakes. Dressing-up has always been great fun to me because it reflected my state of mind. When I was happy and joyful, I wore clothes that made a colorful statement. And so, I very much enjoyed helping ladies groom themselves, mixing and matching outfits and colors that changed their posture, brought a smile to their face and gave them more self-confidence. It was one of my most joyful jobs because the clients and I giggled a great deal about the game of dressing up for whatever occasion. In the theater of life, an appropriate costume made a great deal of difference in an actress's performance.

What else? A short attempt as an interior designer whose skills at displaying furniture and elements of decoration in an environment created the soothing comfort of harmony.

In my adolescence, I studied in a drama school and subsequently became part of an amateur theater group while I was Secretary to the Ambassador of Sweden in Morocco. An acting career was something I contemplated for a while because I thoroughly enjoyed it. As a student in the drama school, I was often selected to perform in certain plays in Classical French festivals, and from time to time, I replaced an ailing professional actress, unable to perform on a particular day in a French soap opera. This was a very happy part of my life because I studied literary texts of drama and poetry in depth and I have always been sensitive to the resonance and harmonious blending of words.

And though I gave my best effort to every job I held—learning a great deal from each of them—I never totally committed myself to any of them on a long term basis.

In the course of those jobs, and between them, the only commitment I had was reading and contemplating. And so, regardless of my professional and family obligations, I woke up every morning at 5 a.m. and spent two to three hours alone with my books and contemplation. In retrospect, I can see now that that's what gave me a relative equilibrium over the years. I needed my regular dosage of spiritual food that helped me distance myself from whatever game I had to perform in the course of the day.

Not to forget that I also became, by necessity, a certified packer by any professional standards. Indeed. Over a period of about twenty-five years, I have lived in eleven different countries. Packing and unpacking was my forte, for nothing arrived broken at its destination.

All this travelling, I might add, made me feel, at times, like a yoyo on a string. But hey, I'm still here. Alive and kicking. If only I could stop kicking and remain still!

And you watched all of this, my beloved God, silently. Without giving me any feedback on what was what. At least, I didn't hear any. And so, like a drunken bee I kept on going my merry, busy way. Apparently it was alright, 'cause I kept going. You made sure of that.

So, these were the activities where I earned money—save that of packer. My other activities were free of charge—in a manner of speaking, for they were certainly charged with emotions. Happy and not so happy ones: housewife—what a word—mother, cook, maid, nurse, chauffeur, teacher, hairdresser, entertainer, accountant, answering service. What else? Oh, God, let's close this!

This is indeed what I did for a living. Literally and figuratively.

Am I advertising myself? Hardly! For, over the past five years, I have removed myself from the rat race, the destructive competitive spirit, the need to prove anything to anyone. Because at long last, I finally realized that it is not what I do for a living, it is who I am that counts.

Please don't ask me who that is. Bear with me. I'm still searching and in the process maybe we will discover it together.

Yes, I have enjoyed all those activities very much. Everything I did in my life, I put my heart and soul in it. Whether I was baking a cake or making a floral arrangement; translating a technical document or interacting with people anywhere in the world. Whether I was nursing my children or entertaining my husband's guests.

Anyway, my reality is now radically different. I do not look for or seek anyone's approval anymore. Save yours, my sweet God. And you tell me clearly, every time, how pleased, or not, you are in me, through my intuition. I have made very drastic changes in my life. A 180-degree turn. I was going to say 360 degrees, but a friend pointed out to me that with 360 degrees I haven't moved. Isn't he clever? Perhaps even with 180 degrees, I haven't moved either. Who knows? I just kept spinning my wheel and chasing my tail.

Let's be serious, now, for a moment. I'm trying to tell a story here!

Yes, all those activities were quite an education to me. When I got bored with one, I went onto the next. Which brings me to my background education. Life, of course. The greatest teacher of all. But I also graduated from "l'Ecole Francaise de Redaction," in Paris. A French School of Letters and the Art of Writing. My Professor, who was member of the Academy of French Letters, told me that I was one of the only three students, out of a thousand, to be urged to write. That was nearly thirty years ago. I never paid heed or followed through. What was I going to talk about? At the time, I couldn't make much sense of my life or explain the turmoil around and within me. What explained the huge gap, the discrepancy, between what I did and what I thought? It didn't make any sense. And if I didn't make much sense to me, I couldn't very well make any sense to anyone else.

Besides, in those days, I was very much influenced by the existentialist movement in France, led by Jean-Paul Sartre and Simone de Beauvoir, who declared God dead, thereby condemning themselves to death. A very nihilistic philosophy, indeed. Though I read all of their books, the belief in God was very strong in me. God had always been that powerful force that manifested itself around and within me; that mysterious force that always pushed me to move forward, enthusiastically. Always enthusiastically.

However, I must give credit to Simone de Beauvoir who greatly influenced my adolescence through the example of her life and her writing. She taught me to dare to walk outside of the beaten path. To dare to think for myself, to be an individual and have the courage to make my choices. Whether those choices were regarded as acceptable or not by society. And so, her own brand of wisdom was quite appealing to me, then.

Wisdom! A word, a quality I have relentlessly pursued for the past thirty-five years. A value dear to my heart. I searched for it everywhere I went, in everything I tried to do, in everything I saw and witnessed. In every book I read: literature, philosophy, psychology, history, sociology. All these fields were abuzz with words and fancy gobbledygook. But where was wisdom hiding its beautiful face?

Wisdom, ever so illusive in the circles in which I revolved, ever so illusive everywhere. But five years ago, I found it in the consciousness of "Ramtha the Enlightened One," who is showering me with it. And one day, I know, it will rub on me, inevitably. For, that is the way he has designed his teaching. He is leading me to that understanding.

Ramtha, a great friend of yours, my beloved God. You sent him to me to learn from him, to listen to you, to pay attention to what you are telling me, ever so subtly. Yes, Ramtha is teaching me to read the signs and hieroglyphics of my feelings and emotions. Your language, my sweet God.

I am getting ahead of myself, here. So, let's go back to my packing status. Twenty-seven years ago, I married a hummingbird. That is, a man in perpetual motion. My husband is constantly running off to another country, sometimes ten or twelve times in any given year. Indeed, one might say that my husband's home is an airplane.

I met him between flights, in Switzerland, where we both worked at the International Labour Office in Geneva. Neutral territory. He coming from the Caribbean and I from Morocco. What a better place than the United Nations for an encounter like this? A few months later, I married him in Washington D.C. That was a bold decision on my part, indeed. For, the moment I made it, I obscurely wondered whether or not I could adjust at once to a new country—the USA, a different language—American, and a new husband whose upbringing, religion, origin and background were absolutely different from mine. Not to forget that I was quite an extrovert, while he was indeed very much an introvert. And as if all that was not enough, on top of it he had a vision too. Really, what was I doing?

I remember when he picked me up at the airport in Washington, D.C. prior to our wedding. He was telling me on the way home that he was not a man of the establishment. Really? He had just joined the World Bank as an Economist!

—You are not? So, why did you join it?

—To understand and change it.

Quite an ambition! And here I was, a simple woman with simple needs. To get married, have children and be happy. And I married a man whose life example was constantly challenging me and forcing me to look within. Not by what he said, but by who he was. Sometimes, I felt like a Don Quixote heading towards the impossible. Yes, I was indeed. Yet, my intuition told me, in no uncertain terms, to settle for the impossible. So I did. The impossible from there on became my daily life sown into the fabric of my being, and to the amazement and often contempt of the people who crossed our path, I too, despite myself, had adopted a vision. To live the impossible, defiantly, proudly, all the while painfully wondering why the world around me did not approve.

Yes, I married a very rebellious man. I discovered that along the way. A conscientious objector who worked as a Senior Economist in both the World Bank and the International Monetary Fund in Washington, D.C. The seats of the mighty and high international finance. After seventeen years, he resigned from his highly lucrative position with all its perks with a big bang and gave all that up to denounce what he deemed to be the abuses of those institutions who were, he said, creating havoc in the economies of the Third World countries. His resignation was in the form of a book entitled *Enough is Enough.*

So, my husband is a crusader of sorts, a lone ranger. An individual challenging the world economic order. Quite a defiance! The earthen pot against the iron pot. A formidable undertaking, to be sure, and a very courageous one at that. It brings to mind a quotation I read somewhere: "To achieve all that is possible, you must attempt the impossible. To be all that you can be, you must dream of being more."

That just about sums up my husband's inner fabric. Living with him for twenty-five years has been indeed most challenging. But isn't it what life is all about? Challenge? It certainly kept me in the heart of action. For his life, his focus, was to overcome, arrive and achieve. From teenagehood onward, his life was a succession of goals that he had set his mind to reach and he did.

He won a scholarship in his native island, Grenada, from the British Government to study at the London School of Economics. He had one chance out of 300 candidates to win that scholarship. He was that one. And as if that was not enough, he subsequently graduated from the London School of Economics with flying colors. Over the years, he was among the first five students out of 20,000 from all the countries of the Commonwealth to graduate with honors.

Yes, my husband was a doer alright. And I? The opposite, a dreamer. All I wanted was to be. I very much resented having to become or do anything. The competitive spirit had always been abhorrent to me, but I had to use it from time to time in my life despite myself. And so, I engaged in competition as fiercely as the next person. However, my emotional needs were of a very simple nature. All I wanted was to lead a peaceful life with my husband and children, and pursue my lifelong hobby without too much fuss: reading and contemplating. I enjoyed reading enormously. Books have been the greatest friends to me, the greatest medicine, the greatest sustaining force in my life. They often launched me in deep contemplation that brought me great joy and inner peace.

But somehow, the world in which I was evolving, the international jet set of Washington, D.C., that was not enough, not by a long shot. I felt like an ugly duckling, tossed in the heart of a very stormy sea that was bombarding my consciousness with slapping waves upon waves of the modern suffragettes, the women's liberation movement. I was not ready to join my sisters in their fight. I didn't have that kind of a fighting spirit then. I was not ready for freedom. Freedom was a frightening word—emotional, spiritual, material freedom—even if sometimes I was ambivalent towards it.

I just wanted to contemplate, from the perspective of my comfortable and highly sheltered life style, the world in its frantic dance, the world-wide dance of the sixties and seventies. The world knocking itself from shore to shore with upheavals, social discontent and revolts at all levels, against the walls built by the controlling forces and established order—I was watching society bursting at its seams.

And I watched it all, uninvolved, detached and materially very secure. But the suffragettes left me no peace of mind. The ever increasing decibels of their uproar, from one year to the next, constantly mirrored back my lack of competitiveness, my lack of guts and my slumbering complacency. More often than not, I felt ashamed and inept. I felt inadequate, because socially, my husband and I also interacted with women who were great achievers and doers. I felt very much like the image of a large poster I had then. In that poster, there was a man sitting on a high stool with his head resting sadly on his right hand and the caption read: "Sometimes I sits and thinks, and sometimes I just sits."

Even my children reflected that uneasiness back to me.

When my children were born, I had decided that I was not going to work for the first five years of their lives, until they were ready to go to school full time. I wanted them to have a solid base of nurturing and security before they were tossed out there. So, with nearly four years difference between the two of them, I stayed at home for ten years.

One evening after dinner, my son, who was about five years old then, asked me out of the blue:

—Mummy, what did you grow up to be when you were a little girl?

Papa grew up to be an Economist, my teacher grew up to
teach me to write and read, but you mummy, you are nothing.
You are just mummy.
When I grow up, he continued, I will be something,
and my friend Sarah will be something too, he said firmly.

I was speechless. It brought tears to my eyes. I took that remark
in for a moment and then replied:

—My sweet, sweet, darling, I grew up to become your mummy.
To love you, to protect you, so that one day you will become a
strong and beautiful man. So that one day you will be someone.

In those days, I hadn't realized yet what a noble and powerful job
it is to be a mother. What a blessed and divine responsibility it is to
raise children.

Mothers, homemakers, should be highly respected. They should
be revered. They are the pillars of society. From one generation to
the next, they have displayed great fortitude. They have always been
compassionate, patient and abused. Abused by the manipulative
programming of the mass media that shows her counterpart, the so-
called miracle woman—"supermom"—who pursues her career and
raises her children at the same time, in a more favorable light.

The mass media signifying to the mother who stayed at home to
raise her children that there was not much glamour in that particular choice. Yet, paradoxically, creating in the heart of both mothers—the one who works and the one who stays at home—some sort
of malaise, some obscure resentment and uneasiness in both cases.
Making both mothers unhappy about their respective situation; a
no-win situation emotionally.

The mass media whose sole aim is to portray every aspect of life, over and over again, as a paradox; always emphasizing the contra-dictory and the extreme. Creating, in the process, a great gap and seemingly irreconcilable differences among people. Keeping alive, in everyone's heart, a perpetual sense of inner and outer conflict. Always reinforcing a sense of guilt and lack of self-esteem.

What a pity, what a sad state of affairs indeed. For, when it comes to motherhood, I personally feel that a career and mother-hood, in today's society, have clearly shown that those two activities are mutually exclusive. Today's confused and bewildered generation is evidence enough to support that fact.

At another time, my daughter, at around the age of eight or nine, also commented:

—Mummy, why a woman is called a woman? A woman is not a man. A woman is a wo.

—Indeed, darling, maybe we should call her a woeperson.

For, a woman is loaded with woes, to be sure. And despite of all that noise and agitation, not much has changed where her social sta-tus is concerned; even today, in the mid-nineties. The flimsy con-cessions afforded to her by men are just a smoke screen. Because today, as much as ever, she is still struggling. She still can't have it all. She has to chose. Her career or her happiness. She doesn't have the same privileges as a man, where, for him, career and happiness go hand in hand. It is not so for her, not by a long shot. However big a name she makes for herself in the world out there, when she goes home in the evening, she still has to cook, clean, wash, fix, nur-ture and whatever else her life style compels her to do. She has to give tirelessly. And I do not want to hear about examples to the con-trary. They are the exception that confirms the rule.

And so, there I was. Very sheltered, with my poetry and philosophy books, day-dreaming and playing with words, like a child with blocks of alphabet letters, while the sixties were raging with the Vietnam War, the Civil Rights Movement, the Women's Liberation Movement, the hippy movement, and society, everywhere in the world, exploding with unrest.

I watched it all from my ivory tower, as though it did not concern me. And, it did not, because then I was not ready or willing to assume my own responsibilities and take a stand. Oh sure, I could debate endlessly, with the best of them, about the ills of society. I could, indeed, criticize very well. But what was my contribution to improve that state of affairs? Well, I was a critic. Yeah, like every hypocrite, I claimed as my own the achievements of others and disclaimed completely the destructive deeds of certain elements of society.

Besides, all those movements and discontentments were revolts against the establishment— that I was immersed in. An integral part of it and benefitted from it lavishly, through my husband's job. I lived my hypocrisy thoroughly. Condemning the establishment, while basking in its "honey pot" as my husband would say.

So, my husband was a doer and I a dreamer. A doer and a dreamer made for a very conventional marriage and quite convenient for him. Very much status quo in that respect. I played his game and tagged along, by choice. Because I loved him and because I enjoyed diversity and travelling, despite my protests to the contrary, despite my protests to all the changes in our daily life.

My choice led to a very enriching and diversified life style. I have experienced, through him, the academic world, when he taught economics at a university; the world of international finance and the United Nations; the world of politics and power, when he was economic adviser to a prime minister. He also represented the IMF in South America, in the capacity of Resident Representative, which is equivalent, in status, to an Ambassadorship. Hence, the diplomatic world.

The experiences, information and knowledge I acquired in the process are truly priceless. For, I always had an intense curiosity about people, everywhere. Their culture, their language, outlook and folklore. I have always marveled at people's diversity and multitudinous ways of self-expression. Whether I was witnessing a voodoo ritual; attending a Hindi festival of light, the "Divali Celebration;" participating in a bacchanal carnival in Trinidad, or witnessing a terribly serious one in Basle, Switzerland.

There was always this curiosity and desire to understand life from their perspective also. But the greatest lesson I have learned, everywhere I went, was that the citizens of any country had nothing to do with the official posture of its politicians. Everywhere I went, what was prevalent to me was our common humanness, the common denominator between us all.

Yes, indeed, I have lived a very diversified life in which I indulged, fully, in my personal hobby. I never lost track of it. Reading and contemplating. For, although I am, in outward appearance, exuberant and extrovert, I am, fundamentally, by nature and inclination, very contemplative.

The happiest moments in my life were spent alone with my thoughts, contemplating and musing about the resonance and consonance of words. Tossing ideas in the air, as one would toss a bonfire that could bloom into a sparkling bouquet of thoughts or, on the contrary, fizz out as utter nonsense.

Words always held a great mystery to me. Not only their sound-vibrations, but their graphical shape also.

And I would take a word and play with it in other languages. French, English, Spanish, or Arabic. Sometimes, I giggled uproariously at my silliness. Because it lead me nowhere; nowhere tangible, that is. For all I know, perhaps I was indeed somewhere and didn't recognize it. Because I lived and evolved in a world where logic and objectivity were the only matters to be taken seriously.

Anyway, these concerns of mine were my own brand of mobility. My personal contribution to society were these private pursuits of mine that brought a lot of joy to my heart. And so, when I interacted with people, this joy and exuberant feeling had a positive effect on other people. It contributed to perk them up. The pursuit of my personal happiness made people around me happy.

So, while my husband was flying all over the planet, I was riding words and flying over landscapes of the mind, quite open to wherever they landed me. I became, that way, very sensitive to poetry. Poetry became, for me, the most profound form of verbal expression, because it was pure imagery. For someone like me, who spent a great deal of time in my imagination, that was indeed a comfortable territory to linger in.

That is why books were very important to me. A sentence, a thought, or even a word would trigger a mechanism that would launch me to great flights and heights and nothing else would matter any longer. I would lose track of time and forget everything else.

Yes, books were, and still are, my best companions. They lead me to Self. To you, my beloved God. To I.

Sometimes, to others, I appeared to be "out of it" as the term would have it, and indeed, I was. Their down to earth and practical outlook and concerns, their object-ivity, were grounding to me, who loved to fly to the unseen: my imagination.

On some level, my imagination has been my only home, my true freedom. In it, everything was possible. In it, there were no blocks or impediments. In it, I was free of any inhibition. As free as in my dreams at night. Day-dreams or night-dreams, there is no difference. They both are non-judgmental worlds.

And so, I can safely say that my greatest joys were derived from my imagination.

And you, dear God, you activated it non-stop. You poured so many hints into it. In my inner adventures, you showed me and highlighted certain avenues and corridors that appeared out of nowhere. I know, you were flying with me. I felt your presence, unmistakably, when large puffs of joy and exhilaration swelled my heart and soul. Thank you, my sweet God, for your companionship. Thank you for carrying me through and raising me above the humdrum of daily life.

Yes, my imagination was my salvation. Through many books, I also sought other imaginations. That is how I became an avid reader. Each book that I opened was like landing in a foreign land. I was excited about exploring it and discovering what it looked like, what it felt like, what it was made of. Discovering it, mirrored back to me my possibilities and my potential. It made me speculate about me. For, in every book that I entered, what I was looking for was me. Only me.

Who am I?

Blessed writer, whose book is right now in my hand, are you the one who is finally going to tell me? Your book got into my hand by design. Every book is a thread that connects me to me, that connects me to you, thoughtful writer. Mysterious consciousness. What you are telling me is no coincidence. I happen to be reading that particular information at the right moment. Because I am ready to receive it and understand it. Every book connects me to the soul that launched it. It makes me realize, feel and know the interconnectedness between us all. It makes me appreciate that nothing and no one is separated from anything or anyone. Separation is an illusion based on a collective misunderstanding.

All my life, I have fantasized and dreamed of becoming a writer.

And all along, in my frustrated and unfulfilled dream, I had failed to realize—I could see that now—that before I could, I had to engage life and experience it. Experience and learn the full gamut of life's tough lessons and arrive at the point where I am now.

Or, are these just excuses not to commit myself, completely, to my dream?

I have lived a full and busy life. I resorted to all sorts of activities in order not to fulfill my dream. Why? Was I afraid of a possible success? Was I afraid of a possible failure? Was I afraid of me?

Today I feel the compelling need to find out, to sort all this out, to take stock and assess it all. To come to terms with it all and reconcile, in me, all the scattered fragments and attempt to see the whole picture. To make peace with that profusion of experiences, joys and sorrows, and so much agitation and stirrings.

What was it all about?

Indeed, it is now time for prospect and retrospect.

So, my beloved God, if I were to appear right now in front of you and you were to ask me:

What have you learned so far? What was the meaning of your life?

Well, from what I have gathered up to now, the theme of my life was "integration." My life very much reflects that fact. I probably came to this world to integrate everything and reject nothing. I am learning, oh God, am I learning how to do that!

To know that there is no such thing as an enemy. The only enemy is projected from within and the thought of having such a perception.

Integration indeed. I was born in Morocco, to Jewish parents. I received a typical French education and schooling. I married a West-Indian, of East-Indian origin, who received a British education and was brought up in the Christian faith. Both he and I were colonized entities. We were both the youngest child of our respective families. And we both always refused to be confined to borders and boundaries. Figuratively and literally. We both regarded the world as our playground and went about the business of living by removing the cliches and labels that society had pinned on our back.

So, who am I?

What is my identity?

I have always been bothered, often intrigued, even perplexed by the question of identity. Through my relentless quest and my persistent probing of this question, prompted by my painful experiences and my compelling need to come to terms with them, I have come to the conclusion that one's:

name,

religion,

nationality,

race,

gender,

profession and

socio-economic background

are just vehicles with which one experiences and perceives life through a unique perspective.

The lessons of that perspective are that one must experience it practically, absorb it emotionally, internalize it spiritually, in order to transcend it and arrive at its ultimate conclusion. The enlightenment of one's soul. For wisdom and understanding do not reside in the intellect, but in the emotions, in the feelings, in the experience. In living life.

Wisdom is the experience of life.

And so, one must go through all this process for the enlightenment of one's soul. One's soul, always exuberant to explore, curious to probe, eager to learn and discover, always ready to play and expand. Forever trying one avenue or another. For no other reason than the sake of learning, the joy of playing, the exhilaration of expanding. For the extraordinary privilege to live.

If I were not humbled by the magnitude of God's presence within me, I may be bold enough to declare that I have resolved the enigma of creation.

What is life all about? It is to live.

And my identity? To be part of it all.

To integrate all that is, for it is an integral part of me.

So, my beloved God, coming back to you. Always. What I have learned so far is that there are two fundamental values in life from which all other values derive. They are LOVE and KNOWLEDGE.

To live, learn, experience, understand, to finally be able to love and embrace it all. I am still working on it. I am actively pursuing knowledge in a school of ancient wisdom, where a great teacher, Ramtha, is patiently teaching me how to interlock all the pieces of my own puzzle, so that I may see the whole picture. The picture in which the shadows purposefully give greater emphasis to the light, and to fully appreciate it all as it is, to recognize it and acknowledge it.

Indeed, the meaning of my life is to integrate it all, to interlock it all, without judgment, with detachment. Simply.

So, who am I, dear God?

I have just answered my own question.

I am an explorer playing hide and seek with my Self—playing hide and seek with you, my sweet God. Splashing in and out of experiences, in order to learn and discover the multifaceted self— the awesome multifaceted You.

Always playing and creating, forever weaving joyous and colorful patterns. To see what comes out of it. To understand what happens with that.

So, my sweet God, maybe I don't need to enter into negotiations with you any longer. For I am starting to sense what you are up to.

LIFE!

All I have to do is come up with a new project and enter into it with confidence and faith that you will back it up, as long as I am jazzed about it, as long as it brings me joy and fulfillment.

I understand, dear God.

I have to flirt with new projects, like a butterfly with different flowers. Flowers and butterflies are equally colorful. Each flower mirrors back to the butterfly a different colour and vibrancy of life.

Meandering, like a butterfly, from one project to the next. Flying over hills and dales, over wild fields and cultivated gardens. So that I may unfold and expand, discover and experience all nuances of colors, all nuances of situations, all nuances of the human condition and marvel at such a display that results from such a journey.

And I am very grateful, my beloved God, that you promoted me to this understanding. For you have become to me my greatest comforter, my confidant, my friend and my strength. You are my inner and outer wealth. You are to me what no words can express.

I surrender fully to the feeling and knowingness that you are directing every step that I take.

What comes next is wait and see. Wait and be.

With You. Always, my beloved God.

CHAPTER III:

The Cosmos Within,
A New Understanding

CONSCIOUSNESS

This week I have had the feeling of living in a state of semi-trance. As though I am here and I am not here.

It seems as if I have entered a new realm, a different reality. Everything around me appears to reflect my state of mind: peaceful, blissful, quiet. A definite quality of silence that is music to my heart. An inner musical background suggesting a state of suspended expectation. Expecting what? It really doesn't matter. I know it will be beautiful, because this feeling also carries with it a sense of detachment. A sense of amusement.

I am basking in a soft, gentle, soothing and tranquil atmosphere. Caressing me all around. I am in a silky cocoon.

Yes, I think I have entered a wonderful territory: my consciousness. And as I walk into it, some of the veils and clouds are lifting off, as though acknowledging my presence and graciously leaving; for I have beamed my acknowledgement of their existence, having recognized their nature and the reason why they were there. They understand that their function has served its purpose and have departed effortlessly, of their own accord, saluting me as they leave.

It is said that "The march of a thousand miles starts with one single step." Indeed. It took me nearly half a century to make that first step. I am happy I did. Now, timidly, and shyly, I am exploring my consciousness, one step at a time, like one who has just entered into a new city, at once unfamiliar and familiar.

My inner city shows signs of interesting times ahead. Somehow, I feel it is hiding a lot of secrets; a lot of surprises, for it has a mysterious history. To say the least. And what about its inhabitants?

Well, some of them I know and enjoy. Others, for some reason, make me uncomfortable. But I plan to understand why, to integrate and befriend all of them, in time, and make peace with them. Make peace with me.

My inner city is also a treasure chest. It has a limitless supply of goods that I may need at any given moment. All I have to do is make the effort to look and retrieve them.

Exploring my inner territory has given me a glimpse of limitlessness.

Whether one's life is barren or rich depends, perhaps, entirely on one's skills as an explorer.

MY GENEALOGICAL TREE

My genealogical tree is a Baobab,
Planted in the middle of the planet Earth,
With its roots plunging deep
Into the core of the Earth and
Its top branches attuned to
The music of the spheres,
Thrusting their off-shoots
To the universe,
In an attempt to decode,
Penetrate and bring to light,
Through the diversity of their shapes,
Forms, texture and colors,
The mysterious and captivating harmony
Of life's concert.

A concert where each instrument,
In the celestial orchestra,
Cooperates naturally, energetically,
To bring forth the dynamism,
Beauty, liveliness and harmony of the whole
In a never ending movement of creation.

And in the never ending dance of the elements,
Mirroring within the universal pool
The sparkles of my own desires and aspirations,
To bring my personal tune to the concert and
Sing, dance, rejoice and create with All That Is.
My genealogical Tree is a Baobab
Also known as Humankind.

HIDE AND SEEK

The sun and the moon play hide and seek with each other.
And in their dance, following their respective journey,
Comes to one's awareness the exuberance and jubilance
Of teeming life under the sun.

And the sweet pause and repose from movement,
The sweet surrender under the watchful guidance of the moon,
Following her dreams, in night meanderings,
It becomes clear that in stillness and silence,
The night, pregnant with dreams, maturing into the dawn,
Fulfills the promise and realization of the day
Mysteriously and playfully concealed by the night.

The day, exploding with the brightness of the sun's rays,
Enlightening and highlighting the beauty,
In the night concealed,
Yet, hinted at by the mysterious light of the moon,
The mysterious darkness over which she is presiding.
Bringing, in the process, the lesson to bear.
To be fully enlightened, to be in knowledge of One
I first have to experience the darkness
From whence all creation mysteriously stems.

Day and Night. Sun and Moon. My God and I.
Mysterious duos.
For, in my own stillness and silence,
Dreaming the dream of genius and simplicity,
The dream of brightness and enlightenment,
In this meandering journey of mine,

I wax and wane in consciousness,
Through darkness and visions,
Pondering and understanding,
Step by Step,
Patiently and purposefully pursuing my own dawn,
My God's light bathing, and showering me
With bright and warming rays,
Pouring into my heart and consciousness,
The knowledge and understanding,
That we are one and the same.

My God and I. Night, and Day,
Rolled into one reality.
I am that which I am.
At the depth of the night,
At the zenith of day,
From one point to the next is the meandering journey,
Is the glorious isness,
Is the glorious knowingness
That I am.

THOUGHTFUL THOUGHTS
OR THE BIRTH OF A PLANET

Over the years, I have contemplated certain thoughts and followed their development, like a gardener watching over the seeds she planted. And one day, what flowed like a river from my pen, were the thoughts I had entertained for a long time. So, when I took pen and paper, the time was right.

I had reached the autumn, the time of harvesting, effortlessly. For my thoughts had matured and were fully ripe to be consumed and absorbed as firm, sweet and juicy fruits.

What a delight to my being to consume a juicy fruit! A fruit vitally nourishing and sustaining my life. What a delight it was to feel the development from the seed of my thought, from the seed of my question, into a fully ripened answer, a fully ripened understanding.

Yes, there are various stages of growth in a thought. It appears as an infant and develops into a child, into an adolescent, into a full-fledged adult.

And if it is followed closely, nurtured, entertained and cared for, it stands as a beautiful entity known as "Wisdom." If not, it wilts and perishes from inner sight. It never reaches the maturation of adulthood. Instead, it disintegrates into sour and acid elements triggering a completely different chain of events.

Yes, our thoughts require a gardener's attention. When neglected they turn into parasites, weeds and obstacles to the rest of the garden.

Everything requires care and love. Everything responds to thoughtfulness.

Thoughtful thoughts, as much as everything else, tended and cared for, lead to harmony and equilibrium in the whole garden.

They lead to completion.
They lead to happy conclusion.

Thoughtful thoughts are thoughts that are full.
They are whole and complete.
They are filled with care.
Whereas thoughtless thoughts are hollow.
They carry in them the emptiness of indifference.
Their essence is thoughtlessness.

A thoughtful thought's journey starts at Alpha,
Climbing all the way to Omega.
Alpha and Omega
The two ends that close the circle
Into a new, and beautiful planet.
Planet: Plan-et
A plan?
E-T? As in Extra-Terrestrial?
An extraterrestrial's plan?
An invisible, intangible plan?
Whose thoughts in fusion became.
Whose churning thoughts
Gave birth to a planet?
Yes, a new planet
A new being, born to a wondrous family
The family of thoughts
Called existence. Existence everywhere.
Existence promoted to light, promoted to life.

A thoughtful Thought
An entity to interact with

To interlace with
Into a silky and smooth union.

A thoughtful thought
To learn from,
To evolve with
To live by.

Thoughtful Thought
I salute you

Welcome into my life!

WEAVING MY WEB

Who am I?
I am both the Spider and the Web.
I weaved a grand and large tapestry
    with my thought processes and
    acting upon those thoughts
    gave definite form and texture
    to each thread in the web.

Each thread is a tangible choice, a state of mind,
    and has a definite flavor to it.
A character all its own.

In my mobile state of beingness,
I may act, interact, or react,
    from the perspective and frame of mind,
    of one thread or the other.

When I say I am,
I am the Spider and
I am also the Threads
    that issued forth from me.
I am my Thoughts and my Deeds.

In the grand scheme of things,
    in the eyes of All That Is,
    The Mega Spider,
I am the child,
A Thread connected to Is.

As a Thread, I went within and unfolded.
I dreamt a dream and became, in turn,
    a Spider in the likeness of God,
    The All in All.

Mirroring back to God his creation
    by extension: Me.
And through me, the unknown is made known.

Everything in life and in nature
    reflects that fact, ad infinitum.

It is the magnificent mechanism of Creation.
The magnificent mechanism of Evolution.
To evolve into Love.
Everything echoes upon itself and
    duplicates itself in a flawless continuum.

THE VISITOR

I was reading a book entitled
Awakened Imagination by Neville,
When Ramtha came to visit.

Oh, he stayed with me for about
The blinking of an eye.
Long enough though,
To drop, in my consciousness, a thought
That went whirling
All the way down to my heart and
There, melted into a feeling.

My sweet and poetic Ramtha,
There is a garden I long to visit.
Your garden.
I want to explore it
With the heart of your consciousness,
For it spells Wisdom to me.

I want to lose myself
In the vast estate of your Wisdom and
Inhale the depth and breadth of its fragrance
        and nuances,
Its subtlety is of such a magnitude,
That I could bask in it forever.
Letting my own consciousness be carried away
By its magnetic and magic flow.

I want to develop a parallel garden,

Containing the same quality,
Only with a different fragrance. Mine.

Won't you, Ramtha, invite me to your garden?

THE PRESENT MOMENT

Speaking in the present tense
I am projecting the future.
What is the future?
A perpetual present in transformation.
A succession of present moments
Running towards their destination
Called evolution.

And in the eternal racing
Of present moments following one another,
I draw the signs
Of my future
Thanks to which
My soul evolves and guesses
The powerfulness of my Consciousness
Without which nothing exists.

My Consciousness creating the world
In imagination
That spreads and extends
Indefinitely
The perimeters of my being.

My consciousness, at one moment
Observes and learns,
At another moment, understands and acts.
And this truth internalized
Fills me with humility,
For at last, I know and recognize

My identity.

Who am I?
I am my Soul
Where plunge all my roots.

My Soul is a platform,
A nucleus,
A receptacle
Containing my experiences and emotions
Transmuted into wisdom and comprehension.

My Soul is a launching pad
From which my desires and aspirations are dispatched,
My prayers and great expectations,
My projects and my will.
All like projectiles
Loaded with my energy
Thrown towards the future
And falling back, a while later,
To their point of departure.
The past returning to the present,
And transformed into realization.

The past and the future
Merging into one and
Becoming, now, my present.

And in the labyrinth
That my thoughts follow
I have joyously assimilated

That now, right now,
Is the only hold I have and know.

What matters, what's important,
Is the present moment.

THE STREET BEGGAR

The most courageous individual I know is the beggar in the street. For it takes a great deal of courage to challenge oneself to a day-to-day, moment-to-moment survival; to dare to face the unknown without an inkling of what the next moment might bring.

A beggar in the street is someone who has stripped himself of worldly possessions and who, at last, finds in his thoughts his warmest clothing, basking from one day to the next in the comfort and security of his Soul.

How else could he possibly continue to strive in his meanderings—for that is probably where life's greatest lessons are found.

Stripped of material possessions, the beggar's contemplations lead him to inner wealth and wisdom. The wisdom that to have nothing is to own everything. Indeed, the material world distracts the individual from himself and distances him from his extraordinary inner kingdom.

Is that what it takes to know Self? For some perhaps. For others, it may require material wealth. To experience, for a fleeting moment, the joy of acquisition. And soon to realize that this too is an illusion.

But materially rich or poor, one's true wealth, one's ultimate wealth, is in the wisdom acquired from all experiences.

Wisdom. That's the ultimate price. That's the ultimate acquisition.

MY AIM IN LIFE

My aim in life is to cultivate my two gardens.
One in the ground, around my house,
The other in my imagination.
Expanding them both, simultaneously.

I want to bring them together into a unified whole
Where the seed in the ground mirrors the idea in the mind
Like two friends, infusing each other with inspiration
To grow and develop,
Through their silent and mysterious journey.
To finally appear, one day,
Miraculously, fully bloomed and happy to be.

And the blessed birth of those two friends,
Saluted in a heartfelt welcome
By the consciousness involved
In the process of bringing them into realization.

Reality. The seed, in the mind.
The idea, in the ground.

Fruit of the imagination.
Fruit of the ground.
Reality made whole and complete.

SADNESS AND JOY

In the heart of sadness
Lies a certain sweetness
That soothes the Soul and
Like a morning dew,
Or a soft falling rain,
Moistens the parched contours
Of one's experiences.

Extreme sadness and extreme joy
Two facets of one coin,
Bringing the same results and
Making the Soul come alive,
Transmuting those feelings into Wisdom.

In the heart of sadness
Lies understanding and compassion.
A mellowing of Spirit.

From the heart of Joy
Radiates unconditional love.

Sadness and Joy,
Compassion and Love,
Emotions that spell
Wisdom.

THE VALLEY OF THE GODS

Last year I went to India, and there, at the foot of the Himalayas, in a village called the "Valley of the Gods," I met a joyful and fascinating Guru, whose mischievous brand of humor was most delightful. Interacting with him for a few days was very inspiring. His joy was so contagious, his laughter so beautiful, that I marvelled to be in the presence of such a happy Entity. He was truly displaying the most light-hearted aspect of life. He is a grand teacher, and teaches to students who come from all over the world to learn and be inspired by his great wisdom.

The last morning I spent with him, I addressed his audience of students. This is more or less what I said.

"Guruji, it has been a great honor and blessing to find my way to your presence. It was meant to be. Over the past few days, you have been a profound source of inspiration to me. God knows I have rejoiced in your divine presence and I am grateful to have had the privilege to bask in your energy field. It is enticing, it is joyful, it is compelling, it is very mischievous! Thank you.

"Your wisdom is most inspiring, for you have captured and daily apply joy—the essence of life. Life, indeed, is a joyful game.

"But sometimes, we get caught in our own game and we get lost and entangled; we tend to forget that it is just a game, an illusion. Very much like the performing actor who, once the play is over, forgets to remove his mask and his costume and continues to play the same performance over and over again. The performance having become his reality.

"If we could look at ourselves, from time to time, as detached observers looking at our performing act, we would surely laugh uproariously.

"Your joy, Guruji, is a sight to behold. With profound respect and love from my Consciousness to Yours, I salute you and I surrender.

"Having reached this point in my personal journey, I have come to understand two important words: focus and surrender.

I now focus on whatever I desire to create in my reality, and I surrender to the subtle voice and calling of "I Am." I recognize that voice as "The Lord God of my Being."

"Lately, I have come to realize that I have never made a mistake in my life, I have never been wrong. Everything I did was for a purpose. When I made a choice, it was a good idea at the time. Whatever I judged it to be subsequently—good or bad—I derived an experience, a knowledge, that later became wisdom. It became one more pearl in the cauldron of my personal experiences.

"If I were to do it all over again, I would not change one single choice, not one single thought of mine. Because all of them combined led me to this point of realization, to this point in consciousness, to this present reality, to this beautiful moment with all of you.

"It was all worth the trouble, the pain and the joy.

"I leave you today with a light and joyful heart, for we don't have to live under the same sky to be together. I carry within me the unforgettable moments we have shared together, I carry with me your beautiful and radiant faces. And so, we will never be separated again, for you are in my consciousness, as I know I am in yours.

And I would like to conclude by saying that I am no longer on a quest, I am no longer on a search. I just am. In the feeling, in the moment, in the now.

This garment, this vehicle called Claude, is constantly fine-tuning and refining itself. This garment, a chrysalis having fun transmuting itself into a butterfly, is the instrument through which "I AM" creates and makes known the unknown.

What is life all about?

It is to live.

My love and blessings accompany you on your personal journey."

And thus ended a magical trip to the "Valley of the Gods." A trip in another place, another time, yet the same consciousness.

Amongst the Guru and his students, I felt at home. I felt a recognition with all of them at first glance. Preliminary introductions were almost superfluous. We were immediately comfortable with one another. Joyfully, effortlessly. As though we had always been together, yet we were seeing each other for the first time.

The hospitality, the graciousness, the warmth and immediate acceptance with which I was greeted by everyone there, was a true match, definitely deserving and befitting of the name of that environment—"The Valley of the Gods."

"Embracing the Spirit of our Source,
we become an expression of it."
—Joan Ocean

CHAPTER IV

Dancing with my Soul

A TOAST TO THE GOD WITHIN

"O my beloved God
You are the song of my Soul
The fire of my Spirit
The morning of my life."

Ramtha

This day, and everyday
I dedicate to You
I salute You, my beloved God
In joy and exuberant energy
For the Glory that is You
For the wonder that I Am.

Claude

THE SOUND OF WISDOM

My personal logo is the key staff.

A human life is an amazing concert. The concert of emotions and experiences. Whether it is a melody, a cacophony, or a symphony, each moment translates itself into resonant vibrations. Harmonious or discordant, depending on whether we are moved by joy or sorrow.

And all these notes, positive or negative, lead us to the same goal: a training in wisdom.

What is the meaning of life? It is to live according to one's rhythm and tune. According to one's own pace.

Ultimately, everything in life leads to wisdom. Anguish and sadness as surely as great exaltation.

A great master, Ramtha, taught me where pearls come from. How they came about.

A pearl, he said, was originally a grain of sand that penetrated inside the oyster, kept spinning within the fragile membrane of the oyster, irritating it to no end and creating, in the process, a discordant tune.

Over the years, the oyster, finally absorbing and integrating that irritation, transmuted it into an iridescent pearl.

A profound emotion, like a grain of sand, contains a potential of evolution, of amazing transformation.

The unique transformation of a grain of sand into a pearl of wisdom.

WITHIN: A MYSTERIOUS WORD

Within. What a mysterious word!
Within starts with a "w."

w.   Double U? Double me?
            One U, sitting on the ground with its siamese twin,
              both with open branches upward.
            So open, in fact, probably the whole universe ventures
              in an out of it all the time.

i.   I. Now, there goes an enigma!
            "I" stands straight and erect,
              with a Dot watching over it.
            Why was the dot added?
            Is the dot a symbol for the Spirit
              thanks to whom "I" can stand straight?

t.   A cross standing on a half circle.
            A cross or a rocky hook.
            The unstable hook of human condition.

h.   A pole and an upside down "U."
            Upside down me? Looking from a different perspective?
            Receiving and aspiring from inner earth
              understanding and nourishment?

i.   Another I. My soulmate?
            Separate from me by the rocky cross "t," and
              enigmatic "h"?

n.   Another upside down "U" Why?
            Are up and down equally meaningful?
            N, when capitalized, becomes two triangles
              open upside down.
            N. For Nothing? No thing? Nothingness?
            No thing as the Void from which emerges Every Thing?
              Waiting to materialize into Some Thing
              Within, a universe of endless probabilities.

Within: An awesome universe
      Containing all possible universes
      Made out of amazing codes and signs,
      waiting to be fashioned from obscurity to bright simplicity.

FLUTTERING FEELINGS BEFORE SLEEP

Over the past few days, I have had the wonderful feeling that I could tap into my mind for any information I wanted, or answer to a question that occurred to me. It is as though my mind has become a radio station. Indeed, at the flip of a button, I could tune in and retrieve the answer. At the flip of a button, it flows like a river.

Come to think of it, over the past year and half, my life has become quite effortless. Everything seems to fall into place. Everything clicks. Something of a domino effect. The natural consequence of a new easy going attitude.

I no longer worry or belabor anything. I surrender to whatever situation presents itself to me and somehow it just takes care of itself.

That's really magic.

Magic to know that I can retrieve any information from an inner record, within a vast library, pulling out a particular book, at the appropriate page, and there is the answer to my question. Is that what the Akashic records are all about?

One thing I have also noticed is that my vocabulary has almost become devoid of "ifs" and "buts." Cumbersome words. Wobbly words, dragging down a load of doubt.

They have been replaced by "Is" and "Indeed." A firmer posture, to be sure. With also a greater measure of faith and confidence in self.

Self. Echoing and ringing.
Suggesting and reaffirming
    everything is there for the taking.

The universe is bountiful.

Equally bountiful for everyone.
All I have to do is open
    the limitless pantry of my imagination and
Pick up what I need
To feed my heart and
Quench my Spirit with experiences.

My Spirit always ready to feast
At the table of new experiences.
My Spirit always turning on the light and
Blinking colorfully at the prospect of a new project.

My beloved God, let's create a new project!
Let's see.
I could start to develop wings.
Though my thoughts go faster than they could.
So, that's not it. That won't do.

How about travelling through time
Backward and forward
Rearranging the past and sketching the future?
No, that's not it either.
We want to experience NOW.

Oh, well, let's sleep on it and
Catch a fluttering train
The train of thoughts
Riding through the night and
See at what new city we arrive in the morning.
What new reality the morning will bring.
Good night!

THE MUSE AT PLAY

Playful and unpredictable,
The Muse circled around my imagination,
Laughing and teasing no end.
Sometimes, crackling up a large bonfire,
She launched her sparks in all directions
Yet, neglected to hand me a net
To catch them all.
Rather negligent of her. Wouldn't you say?

Anyway, I caught what I could with my earthly fingers,
The rest disappeared, somewhere, within my inner spaces.
I will find them, somehow, with the right radar.

Not only that. She also beams her light and
    throws her sparks on my lap while I meditate.
Is she doing it on purpose?
As everyone knows, while meditating
One doesn't move.
Muse or no muse.
Though I do ask her to come back when I'm through.
I do ask her to hold those thoughts,
    suspend those ideas and serve them back to me,
    unchanged, at the appropriate time.

My request makes my muse laugh heartily.
My muse finds that very amusing. Am-using?
My beautiful Muse doesn't understand what "appropriate" means,
    every moment is the right moment to her.

Anyway, it is a known fact that Muses are fickle
    and unpredictable.
Mine doesn't care what I happen to be doing and where
    I am at any given time.
She appears in the oddest moments and strangest places.
For instance, while talking to my boss,
    she blinks at me daringly and smiles defiantly.
Now, really! How could I listen to his instructions and
    answer her imperative call at the same time?

Or while sitting on the toilet bowl. Of all places!
Tapping her forefinger on my shoulder,
Having no qualms about whether or not
I have pen and paper, to write then and there.

Anyway, for all her unpredictability, I enjoy hooking my cart to
    her wings.
It is so much fun zigzagging and zooming
    from one idea to the next, and
Catching them like blinking fireflies,
Appearing out of nowhere,
In a midnight background.

TAP DANCING

I do not know how to tap dance with my feet,
But I sure know how to do it with my heart.
And the steps of that dance are feeble imitations
    of my joyful inner exaltations.
Can you hear the cadence and balance of those steps
    and perceive, at the same time,
    the rhythmic meanderings of my Spirit,
    drawing graceful geometric designs in open skies?

Absorbing and embracing, arms stretched
    and ears finely attuned
    to the celestial music of the spheres
Merging and blending with that music
    in a revolving movement of myself
    spiraling and creating, endlessly,
    elevated and exuberant sound waves.

What kind of music does my being emit?
It emits lively and harmonious tunes
    of joyous moments captured in eternity.

A music that translates into the exuberant
    tap dancing of life.

I COULD FLY

I could fly,
I could dance,
I could swing and jump.
Revolve and zigzag.
I could zoom up and
Dive down,
Splashing my energy all around.
Everywhere.
Like a drunken soul,
Drunk with life,
Immersed in joy,
Dripping with energy,
Vibrating with exuberance,
Giggling and laughing,
Expressing the jubilant weightlessness
    of my being
And running with the speed of light
Leaving traces of energy
Across the happy sky, that read:
I'm Alive!
Like a meteor.
Indeed.
I could fly.

THOUGHT RECORDER

They have not invented yet
A recorder for the Thoughts.
That's too bad!
If they could record mine,
They would be charmed by their harmony and
Melodious sound waves
Wrapping them with a soothing,
     peaceful and soft envelope.
The texture feels like a rose petal,
Translucent, pleasing, teasing to the senses,
Which, in turn, will make them alert,
Happy and lively.

Ah! If they could record
The sound vibrations of my Thoughts,
They would be able to travel with me
To the far reaches WITHIN and
Together, exuberantly,
We would be able to dance
The lively and graceful dance of life.

THE COMPOSER

I am a song, a lively melody
That my God uttered sweetly into being.
My dancing notes and feelings
Meander in and out of the mighty Composer
Who breathed them into play.

As a melody, I travelled far and wide
Spreading around my frequency,
Leaving behind echoes of my being
That vibrated in some hearts
And left no trace in some others.

I am a hearty song,
From a long repertoire,
Passionately written
By a mighty Composer
Whose only aim
Is to sing joyfully
The song of life.

I am the composition
Reflecting back to the Composer
The harmonious sound vibrations
Uttered in the airwaves
And recognized everywhere
By the name and sound
That I am that which I am.

IN THE HEART OF THE WOODS

I want to live in a cottage, in the heart of the forest,
Where I will make merriment with my neighbors,
　　the wild geese and the chipmunks.

The crickets will come to my doorsteps,
　　chirping their heart away;
　　I will join them, singing a tune or two.

The gentle wind will carry
　　the soft murmurs of the brook nearby,
　　calling me for a visit,
　　for it has a secret or two to share with me.

And my heart will joyfully swell at the secret that tells me:
　　I am an extraordinary part of all that lives,
　　an integral part of All That Is,
　　for my Consciousness has been made aware of that secret.

And, for a brief moment, my CONSCIOUSNESS,
　　like a lightbeam,
　　highlighted the exuberance of life,
　　like an amplifier, echoed the music of each element
　　that strives, flies, runs, pulsates, expands, sings, dances,
　　around me, within me,
　　EVERYWHERE,
　　in a compelling, and never-ending expression of LIFE.

A MEDALLION OF LIGHT

A medallion of light
Hanging on the wall
Came to play with me one day.
When I moved, it moved.
When I stopped, it stood perfectly still.
When I got up, it went to the ceiling.

Now, what was this?
I had no trinkets, jewelry
Or blinking metal on me
That could play games
With the morning rays.

Oh, it was such a lovely
Medallion of light!
Paying me a visit of courtesy.
Or, was it a Consciousness
Prying on my privacy?
Or, better yet, an apparition
Delivering an explanation.
An apparition cheering me with its light
For it was playful and bright.

No matter, it was there for a reason.
Did I attract it?
Or did it come to deliver a message?

And what was the message? The message was
To pay attention and recognize

To recognize and acknowledge
To learn to read
Learn to decipher the signs
Tangible and intangible
Material and immaterial
They all contain a symbol.

Each symbol has a meaning and
The meaning is the answer within the question.
The word "Why" transmuted into "Explanation."
To explain—ex-plain.
An ex question with an answer made plain.

Explanation: Ex - plan - nation
An ex nation with a plan?
Ex - pla - nation
An ex nation at play?

Indeed. There is within me
A great nation of Thoughts
Ex and current
Past and present.
Playing and planning.
Twisting and turning.
Meandering and travelling.
Flying and landing
Into this understanding.

I understand
Beautiful Medallion of Light
The message of your apparition.

I read you.

Thank you for exhibiting your light
Thank you for manifesting that understanding
Showing me that what matters is
To feel and know
Know and understand
Understand and appreciate
Appreciate and Love
Love and live.

Thank you Medallion of Light.

Oops! It just disappeared!
Bon voyage, messenger of joy
Bon voyage, Messenger of peace and good tidings!

May you become
The welcome visitor in every home
And may all closed curtains
Open wide and let you enter
In hearts and minds,
In love and understanding.

Bon voyage, Medallion of Light!
Messenger of hope
Don't be a stranger, now
Come back to visit soon
To play and chat
To play and highlight.
Au revoir!

CELEBRATION

Today I celebrate life.
What is life?
Life is exuberance. It is energy jubilantly bursting forth.

Life is quiet anticipation. And joyous expectations.
Expecting what? The free and wild flow of the next moment,
    and the next, and the next, in an **eternal present**.

Life is the sweet feeling in the midst of sadness,
The fluttering nostalgia in the heart of ecstasy.
Joy and sorrow are the two ends that close the circle,
Melting with one another in a unified pool
Within which one evolves, from one moment to the next,
From one emotion to the next.

And all the feelings and emotional ripples,
Spreading and expanding, extending wider and further,
The perimeters that encircle one's being
In an ever widening universal pool
Until one's Consciousness reaches, incorporates and
    encompasses the whole universe.
Until one's Consciousness is at one with All That Is
Until One, suddenly, in a moment of illumination
Is the spontaneous pulsation of a bird in his flight and
    the "coquetry" of a flower preparing to bloom,
The bewildered expression of the beggar in the street and
The royal pride of the king in his palace.

Until one is the crystal laughter of a child and

The tree whose branches sway in the wind.
Until one is the wind bending and ruffling furiously
    the striving vegetation in a stormy temper tantrum,

And the rainbow, smiling colorfully, afterwards,
Appearing miraculously and bringing the lesson to bear:
The storm begat the Rainbow.

THE THOUGHTFUL GARDENER

I am blossoming, beloved Ramtha.
I am unfolding, I am growing.
I feel it.
I feel the awareness of it,
Like an electrical current shooting
Through my entire being.

In all this focus and contemplation,
In silence and stillness,
Unbeknownst to me, I was germinating,
I was developing and expanding and
Now, my head has pushed its way out of the dark,
Above the ground.

Boy, all this light, all of a sudden, makes me dizzy!
I have to get used to it.
I will, and it won't make me blink or become disoriented.

And while all this mysterious work was taking place,
My impatience was telling me I was doing nothing.
I wasn't going anywhere.

But you, Mighty and Noble Gardener,
Oblivious to my impatience,
You kept sprinkling me steadily and purposefully
With the right dosage of thoughts,
Moistening my heart, my imagination,
My Soul and my Spirit with love,
Imbibing my whole being with expectations,

Fertilizing me with your Wisdom.
Breathing and infusing my will with your energy.

And now, I am suddenly becoming aware of You.
You have nurtured me into waking up and
Now I can see you see me.

What a reflection on you, Beautiful Gardener.
For you to look at me
For me to look at you and see me.
What a reflection on you, Magic Gardener,
For me to respond and harmonize with your intentions.

I am ready to dance, Ramtha,
I am ready to soar and fly
In that compelling territory called Joy.
In that magnificent land called Experience.
In that enigmatic and wondrous reality called Life.

Today I know, with a knowingness never experienced before,
That the great work has begun.
The great work about the business of awakening,
Living and appreciating.
The great work about the business of recognizing and
    Acknowledging. The great work about remembering.

I remember you, Ramtha.
I salute you, Mighty Gardener,
With a recognition on a par with your efforts.

WAKING UP

This fine morn, I woke up with puffs of joy radiating from my heart. Did I travel in a wonderland during the night? I must have! Because this morning I feel strong, with a comforting sense of direction. A quiet sense of assurance that makes me feel my steps are purposeful.

Somehow, I know where I am going.

My purpose is to learn and to share my learning and understanding, as it unfolds, with others, through writing.

Suddenly, I no longer feel this sense of hollowness inside, the sense of groping in the dark that I've had all my life. Going through the mechanical motions of life, like an animated doll, whose key was turned on to make a few zigzag steps, totally unaware of herself.

Suddenly, all the down-to-earth routines that were my life up till now, vanished and gave way to a new vista. Enveloping me with a warm and secure feeling of integration, of self-alignment.

An evenness of being.

And the animated doll has become an individual, alive, endowed with a strong willpower. The will to learn and understand. To understand and to know. To know and to love. Unconditionally.

A knowingness that says: "It is not I who do these things, but the Father within." Indeed, I have a strong sense that what comes from my pen is the God within talking to me, talking through me. And how do I know that? Because the words flow from my pen effortlessly. They flow like a river. As I am writing, I am, as it were, listening to my God talking to me, explaining to me, making sense of it all.

My beloved God, I am so grateful that no words can match the feeling I have right now.

I am alive and filled with your presence within and around me.

Indeed, I feel fulfilled. Truly for the first time.

Thank you, my beloved God, for the powerful sense of trust and faith I feel about your blessed presence in me. Your blessed guidance that makes me sense the purpose of it all, with an awareness that is carrying me as though in a weightless way. An awareness that is lifting me out of life's humdrum into a softer and safer environment.

In that environment, all of a sudden, everything feels different. The vista and perspective are lighter. It is as if I had been confined in an eggshell all my life and I burst it open.

How wonderful! How roomy!

Wow! What a view!

The world suddenly appears so spacious, so limitless, so colorful and bright!

Wow! What an amazing diversity of things around!

Human beings, animals, vegetation, minerals, a million kinds of variety in each. And I didn't see any of that before?

All of that was just faint shadows. Talk about blindness! Not to have seen any of it. Not to have appreciated any of it, because I took it all for granted. Because I had colored it with the eyes of boredom.

And now, all I have to do is shake the broken shell from me and move forward.

Go and experience it. Go and look at it, truly.

Go and live it all. For the first time, authentically, joyfully.

The adventure now begins.

Claude walking in wonderland and seeing with the eyes of Alice. Marvelling at the grandiosity and majesty of nature all around. Of nature within me.

Having arrived, in my meandering thoughts, through this long journey of mine, in front of a door, pushed ajar, and inside made contact with Self.

The nameless, timeless, limitless Self. My beloved God, who had been patiently, wisely and lovingly waiting for me, all along. Watching and guiding me while I was lost in the woods the entire time until I found my way out.

Self. Smiling silently, lovingly grateful that I made it to the door. The only door. Wrapping and surrounding me with an all encompassing energy of love.

Self, irradiating, wide and far, the powerful understanding that I AM.

DIVINE WEDDING

I am in a romantic state. A mood of love has overcome me, enveloping me in an atmosphere of quiet wonderment. I am in love with my divine husband: the Lord God of my Being.

Since last night, I have felt a powerful, protective envelope encompassing me. An extraordinary shield, a huge circle surrounding me in an invisible way.

Within that invisible, roomy cocoon, profound feelings of gratitude and quiet joy are welling up in my heart, overwhelming feelings of love that make me want to hold the universe in one single embrace.

I am caressed by a sentiment of tranquillity that is carrying me by a thousand floating feelings, blissfully undulating within my inner domain. My new home, completely renovated and renewed by this divine wedding.

I am the bride of the Lord God of my Being who has lovingly led me to this new dawn.

And my grateful tears are falling softly, as a gentle and soothing rain. Drop by drop coming down and perching themselves like sparkling diamonds on my inner petals. My petals about to unfold and bloom into a new bouquet of thoughts.

I am over-awed by the wonderment of it all, and I know no words to express my gratitude, except these tears of recognition and acknowledgement. These tears of surrender whispering to my Soul: I am free at last. I am freed by a mighty force called Love.

Throughout the night, fully and wholeheartedly consuming the passion of experiences, where apprehension gave way to surrender, hesitation to delight and intertwining feelings, leaving behind uncertainty and doubt, at long last, I reached, at dawn, a point of unity. Unleashing the creative impulses. Pregnant with promises of the future.

Coming full circle, I have arrived, after a long and passionate journey, at my initial point of departure. A single-minded explorer who has gathered, along the way, feelings, many emotions and experiences. After absorbing much understanding, I have finally returned home to my Bridegroom, to the God within, celebrating and saluting in unity this new and glorious dawn.

My wedding night, akin to the passions of life's experiences, led me to reach this new dawn, fully spent physically, and blissfully liberated upon waking up.

My new dawn, a graduation day, where a new Understanding has been bestowed upon me. My rightfully earned diploma that gives me access to the next step in evolution.

And now that I am awake, I can lean back and fully enjoy this honeymoon, this crowning graduation, with You, my sweet and divine Husband. Basking for a while in the wonder of the moment before contemplating my next adventure, my next reality. The next phase of my life in which I will again plunge, head on, into the unknown.

"Making known the unknown," the fundamental principle of life that involves perpetually travelling through the obscure corridors of Lord Mystery, and boldly unveiling them one by one. Penetrating and deciphering the secrets of Lady Enigma and bringing them triumphantly to light for everyone to contemplate.

Mystery and Enigma, the most inspiring and evolving couple, always extending an Invitation to be approached and understood, yet very circumspect to those without the right motives.

Lord Mystery and Lady Enigma, playing hide and seek with us, challenging us passionate explorers to discover their nature.

And as long as the breath of life animates us, we take on the challenge. Finite minds contemplating infinity.

Infinitely gathering and rearranging, exploring and blending countless probabilities, giving birth to endless outcomes. Extending further and wider the possibilities of this wondrous and tantalizing couple. Mystery and Enigma, forever throwing their rays of light for us to ride.

Blessed and Divine Wedding day, I am that which I am in the eternal pursuit of creation, in the never-ending dance of life.

Dancing with my Soul eternally.

ABOUT THE AUTHOR

I was born in Morocco when it was still a French colony and received a typical French education and schooling, though I was born to Jewish parents in an Arabic land.

Because of the unique circumstances of my upbringing—being exposed to three distinct and conflicting cultures: French, Jewish and Arabic—I experienced a formidable identity crisis.

I couldn't relate to any of the three cultures, yet I intuitively felt that each was sewn into the fabric of my being. To deny any one of them was to mutilate a unique facet of my character.

For I embody, firstly, the Jewish values of intense curiosity, an unquenchable thirst for knowledge and understanding, a profound need for justice and fairness, indeed an urgent need to make sense of the world and transmute chaos into harmony.

Secondly, I feel I am characterized by French psychology—Cartesian in nature—based on logic and reason, that believes only in the tangible and concretely demonstrable. Indeed, the high refinement of a French education and manners like pure marble, polished and cold, are inbred in me.

And last, but not least, the extraordinary Moroccan values of intuition and warmth, of gracious hospitality and spontaneousness, in one word, the language of the heart, abide deep within.

This melting pot of characteristics created, over the years, a formidable identity crisis culminating when I reached my teenage years. That was the starting point of my lifelong search for my identity.

My passion to integrate and balance the three cultures in my life led me to travel around the world searching. In thirty years, I resided in eleven different countries from the Middle East to

Europe, from India to North and South America and the Caribbean. Always, the core motivation of my life was to reject nothing and no one, to absorb and integrate everything. My life indeed reflects this—I knew that only through integration could I become whole and view the world as an integral part of myself.

This is why I have chosen to evolve within International circles. As a translator, I have interpreted, literally and figuratively, the experiences of my life into a unique understanding. Everything I discovered and experienced was indeed a projection of my Being. From lack of identity to self-discovery, I came to realize that the world was part of my identity, for it existed only insofar as I acknowledged its existence.

My book is an account of my outer and inner journey which led to the conclusion that one's identity has nothing to do with one's name, religion, nationality, race, gender, profession, or socio-economic background. These are just vehicles that we use to experience life. Indeed, the point of reference for any individual, the root of one's identity, is one's Soul.

One's Soul, the launching pad, the springboard, the authentic "nationality," that compels us to act and react in a unique manner, projecting back to the world a unique flavor, a unique behavior, a unique state of Being.

One's Soul embodying a special blend of choices and emotions, constantly splashing in and out of experiences, to finally arrive at a particular point in consciousness, a particular spot in understanding what life is all about.

And what is life all about?

It is to live. Without judgment, without inhibition, spontaneously, for the sake of evolving, for the extraordinary privilege to live.

To be able to achieve and enjoy, at long last, God's gift of life:

"Dancing with my Soul."

—written by the author, Claude Ohayon-Budhoo